TEN
Yorkshire
MYSTERIES

TEN
Yorkshire
MYSTERIES

TRUE TALES
FROM THE COUNTY

Len Markham

COUNTRYSIDE BOOKS
NEWBURY, BERKSHIRE

COUNTRYSIDE BOOKS
3 Catherine Road
Newbury, Berkshire

ISBN 1 85306 376 2

Designed by Mon Mohan

Produced through MRM Associates Ltd., Reading
Typeset by Paragon Typesetters, Queensferry, Clwyd
Printed by J.W. Arrowsmith Ltd., Bristol

CONTENTS

MAJOR TOWNS and CITIES
of
YORKSHIRE
Including place-names from
TEN YORKSHIRE MYSTERIES

Muker
Thwaite
SWALEDALE
Feetham
Reeth

HARROGATE

LEEDS
BRADFORD
HUDDERSFIELD
Hartshead
Old
Snydale
BARNSLEY

SHEFFIELD

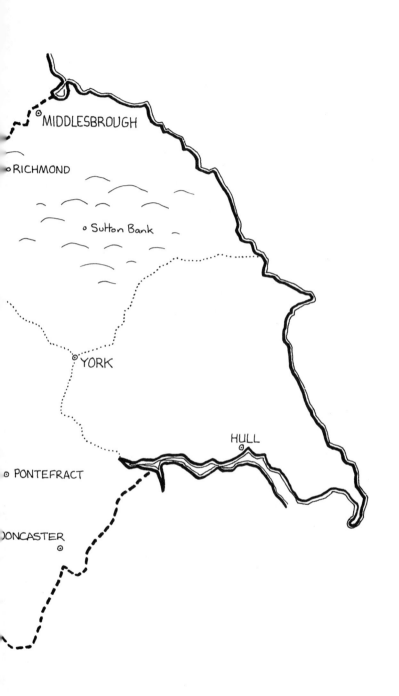

MIDDLESBROUGH

RICHMOND

Sutton Bank

YORK

HULL

PONTEFRACT

DONCASTER

INTRODUCTION

This absorbing collection of authentic Yorkshire stories garners a compelling and sometimes chilling mixture of violence, intrigue and mystery. Recording grisly, unsolved murders, unfathomable hauntings, an unidentified corpse and one unaccountable disappearance, these tales attract hypothesis and conjecture to this day.

The mysteries span the county, recalling savage killings in Middlesbrough, Upper Swaledale and Old Snydale, unexplained ghostly happenings in Leeds, Brighouse, York, Barnsley and Pontefract, the discovery of a still anonymous body near Sutton Bank and, far from these shores in the icy waters off the North Cape, the enigmatic loss of the Hull trawler *Gaul*.

The background for these accounts has been drawn from singularly unimpressionable people, traditional bluff Yorkshire folk not given to fantasy, exaggeration or misrepresentation. So, as extraordinary as the stories are, they have a heightened veracity although obscured by time, a labyrinth of tortured detail and in some cases by deliberate distortion and obfuscation.

In presenting the following pages, I have attempted to record the details of these exceptional cases lucidly and succinctly, without gratuitous drama. The facts and the testimonies of witnesses, I believe, need no gilding, although in parts I postulate theories. Suffice to say that these suggestions are all my own and, far from solving riddles, they may only add to the mysteries which remain among the most intractable in Yorkshire history.

Len Markham
Barwick-in-Elmet
Autumn 1995

Richard Lionheart sought heavenly salvation in the Holy Land, leaving behind a divided nation.

THE GRAVE OF ROBIN HOOD

The mystery of the outlaw's grave, 1247

What has always been regarded as the grave of Robin Hood lies near Hartshead in West Yorkshire, on land owned by the dynastic Armytage family, whose own history now seems entwined with the legend's recent past. The grave's appearance today is one of neglect and abandonment; overgrown and anonymous, it is a remarkably sad monument to whoever lies below. That it should have become associated with unsavoury rituals, a focus for black magic activities and a site for alleged hauntings is a major part of this mystery.

If, as most scholars agree, the character we know as Robin Hood was merely an amalgam of several charismatic robber chiefs, it does not explain how the outlaw himself has become so famous. Given this fame it is surprising then that the grave of this mythic, fêted folk hero should suffer such neglect.

The story of Robin Hood, the folk hero, was born in that misty and turbulent epoch forever associated with Richard Lionheart and the Crusades. While Richard sought heavenly salvation and the blood of the infidels in the Holy Land, his brother John's tyrannical rule must

Traditional images of Robin Hood.

have produced a number of popular, robber chiefs outlawed by their opposition to the English king's caretaker. The product of this tyranny, Robin Hood, has had his historical bedrock blown away by centuries of romantic hyperbole, despite some tantalising references to his exploits quarried from some normally reliable sources in ancient texts and chronicles.

The historical figure, Robert of Huntingdon, who does have some factual credence, can be separated from the popular folk hero and for that period in our country's past his story is not untypical of many of the landed gentry. As the dispossessed and outlawed heir to the earldom of Huntingdon, he waged a guerilla war against Prince John and his representative, the Sheriff of Nottingham, until his triumphal reinstatement by the king and his marriage to a royal ward, the Lady Marion. All was exploit and adventure until his death at the hands of his kinswoman, the Prioress of Kirklees, in 1247.

Motivated, it is said, by her sick cousin's opposition to the religious orders, Elizabeth de Stainton, in consort with her lover-accomplice, the priest Sir Roger of Doncaster, plotted the death of Robert under the pretext of nursing him back to health. Following the accepted medical practice of the age, she prescribed venesection and deliberately opened an artery so that her patient would bleed to death. But before he died he called for his lifetime companion, Little John.

'Bring me my bow and let me shoot once more!' he implored.

'At what would you shoot?' asked Little John.

'My grave, dear friend! Bury me wherever this arrow falls.'

Some 750 years later, the grave lies largely forgotten

and overgrown in the private estate of the Armytage family. Its anonymity and abandonment is all the more remarkable in this modern era where themed historical exploitation is the norm. The grave of 'Robin Hood' could be a national monument, a place of pilgrimage, garlanded, revered and honoured in an annual ceremony of thanksgiving for a life that enriched the nation. Instead, it is abandoned to the twilight realm of mysticism and the occult. Why should this be so? Does the answer lie in the imprecations of Little John, who, on the death of his murdered friend, cursed the priory of Kirklees forever?

Throughout his life, Robert constantly challenged abuses within the church. The corrupt Abbot of St Mary's in York, where the monks indulged in a life of indulgence and debauchery, became his especial enemy and there is no doubt that his denunciations of the closeted and cosy life of luxury and privilege angered and provoked the wrath of holy ordered hedonists everywhere. A firm motive for the murder is, therefore,

A medieval woodcut illustration showing 'Robin' distributing largess.

well established, the actions of the wicked Prioress being further incited by a long-standing grudge harboured by her lover priest. At the age of 87 on the 24th December 1247 (although the date is uncertain), he was murdered. According to legend, his expiring body was cursed by his murderers, he died without the sanctity of the last rites and his body was interred in unconsecrated ground, some 650 yards from the priory gatehouse. This combination of events, culminating in

'You shall be sworn, that you will never tell lies again' – Robin Hood admonishing the priests.

An Edwardian photograph showing the ornate cast iron surround which protects the grave at Kirklees Park. (Halifax Libraries)

the deconsecration of the entire area in 1539 at the time of the Dissolution of the Monasteries, is cited by some as the root of the current enigmas.

It is difficult to review the history of this place with a dispassionate eye; such is the ethereal, shadowy, controversial and downright frightening nature of the subject, that I will endorse nothing nor draw any conclusions, other than to note that here indeed is a monumental mystery.

The one unshakable truth in the whole affair is the certainty that the priory of Kirklees was demolished on the instructions of Henry VIII. At the time of the Dissolution it had seven nuns, who were dispersed. According to some ancient records, three of them – Cecilia Topcliffe, Joan Leverthorpe and a pregnant novice, Katherine Grice – took shelter in a building opposite the old priory. After giving birth, the novice is

16

said to have committed suicide by drowning herself in Nunbrook. Other than foundations, little remains of the priory buildings. The only standing structure is part of a gatehouse. This is not, as has been assumed, the original one – Pevsner asserts its post-Reformation origins. So much for the plain facts. What of the legends and the myriad subsequent claims of hauntings and even visitations by vampires and the rest?

The brutal murder is given a flimsy credence by ballads and ancient chronicles. An account dating from 1677 attests to the death in a riding accident of Sir John Armytage 'just by Robin Hood's grave.' The allusion is that the gentleman was somehow thrown from his horse by dark forces. In the 18th century, an inscription was placed on the outlaw's burial place:

'Hear underneath dis laitl stean,
Laz robert earl of Huntingtun;
Ne'er arcir ver as hie sa geud,
An pipl kauld im robin heud;
Sick utlawz az hi, an iz men,
Vil Ingland nivr si agen.
Obit 24 Kal. Dekembris 1247.'

This replaced an earlier medieval cross mentioned in Camden's *Britannia*, a survey of the British Isles written in Latin and published in 1586. The cross was apparently moved during the Reformation to Hartshead churchyard, where it may still be seen.

For the last 300 years or so, the grave site has been the focus of superstition, attracting those with a fascination for the supernatural, like moths to a flame. Local attitudes to it were summed up in the 1812 publication *Land of Lost Content – The Luddite Revolt*. This reported,

The gravestone in the Hartshead churchyard said to have been moved here at the time of the Dissolution of the Monasteries. (Barbara Green)

18

'The Armytage family lived over the brow of a hill on a splendid site once occupied by Benedictine nuns. It was called Kirklees. There was more than an insularity which set the mansion apart. There was a mystery about it which local people only reluctantly tried to penetrate. The mystery was helped physically by the thick shroud of trees that surrounded the place, and it was sustained by local tales of ghosts and prioresses and nuns and the death of Robin Hood, whose grave is so imperturbably marked as lying within Kirklees grounds in spite of any facts history might suggest to the contrary.'

Such fascinating references attracted trespassers, for the grave was, and remains, on private land. Even the landowner himself was, around this time, lured to attempt an exhumation. Sir Samuel Armytage found nothing, but still the visitors came. In the early 19th century, the tomb was desecrated during construction of the Lancashire – Yorkshire Railway, navvies investing the sepulchral slab with curative properties and chipping off pieces to place under their pillows to alleviate toothache! Tourists have been secretly visiting the grave ever since. It has continued to moulder and disintegrate, its malevolent reputation and its linkages with obscure groups becoming more pronounced. Clandestine vigils at the graveside have increased and there have been several documented, but until now unpublished, first-hand accounts of ghostly encounters. With the permission of one of the visitors, a local man, Roger Williams of Bradley, I quote the following:

'I have had two experiences near the grave site up at Kirklees Park. The first was in the early sixties while walking up there with a friend (who doesn't want to be named). It was the first time that I had seen the grave and as we were walking away from it I saw a figure standing about 20 yards away to my left and to the left of the grave site. Well, we had air rifles with us and in that autumn of 1963 that was a no-no, and I immediately thought it was the gamekeeper. But then this figure started to move towards us and I saw it was a woman. I say move, because she seemed to kind of glide towards us and there wasn't any noise of feet walking over the dry fallen leaves, twigs and dry bracken on the ground. As she came to within 5 yards of us we saw her very clearly. Her eyes seemed very dark and she looked mad, annoyed at us. Then she moved on past us; didn't look back, then she was gone. We realised that what we had just seen wasn't a real person at all and it shook us up a lot. It was 2.30 pm and it was a bright sunny afternoon.

'The second time I saw the apparition was in 1972. Again in the autumn. I am a musician and my bass guitarist, Phil Marsden, asked me if I knew where Robin Hood's grave was, and would I take him up there to see it. It was Saturday afternoon. The day was chilly but nice. As we were coming away from the grave, I bent down to fix my shoelace. Then Phil said 'Hey Roger, there's a woman coming.' As I looked up I saw the exact same thing as I had seen that day in 1963. Except this time she stopped not six feet from us. I'll never ever forget the experience. She wore a long off-white dress kind of squarish around the neck with long sleeves. The dress had some sort of pattern to it. But again it was her eyes I remember most: dark, mad, set in her pale face. She looked at me and then at Phil so close I could have touched the hem of her dress as I was still crouched down messing with my shoelace. Then she moved on right past us and was

20

Roger Williams drew these two sketches of the apparition he saw at Kirklees Park.

gone. Well, I thought Phil was gonna drop right there, cos he'd gone really white. We got out of the wood very fast.

'Footnote: Both times that I saw this apparition things started to happen in my house. Noises, bangings and a feeling like I was being watched. And the lad I was up there with in 1963 got the same. So did Phil Marsden in his home. So you see, I really would advise anyone to be very careful. Better still, not to go up there till the site has been blessed.'

Following his experiences, Roger Williams drew two sketches of the woman he had seen.

Other people have seen terrifying apparitions at the graveside, notably Barbara Green of Brighouse, who founded the Yorkshire Robin Hood Society in 1984. I quote from her detailed account:

21

'Then I saw them, at first as flittering, amorphous forms merging with the murky mists which coiled ever thicker and malevolently round the trees. Two distinct forms that I had no trouble recognising as the Prioress of Kirklees and her lover, Red Roger of Doncaster... Like a bat she hung there for what seemed an eternity, her black nun's robes flapping eerily while her eyes flashed red and venomous and her teeth bared sharp and white between snarling blood red lips. Her lover, Red Roger, remained behind her, his crimson clad figure contrasting drastically with her black one. True to his name, he was like the personification of Mephistopheles... for not only was he dressed in startling, murderous red but his hair was wild and ginger and stood out of his head like rampant flames...'

In recent years, the Yorkshire Robin Hood Society has, in the light of such dramatic incidents, tried to stimulate debate, to arrange public access to the site and, all these years later, to bestow upon Robin a Christian rest. All requests for discussions on negotiating a public right-of-way have, however, been refused and, unaccountably, all attempts to have the grave blessed have been thwarted.

In 1989 an application was made to Lady Armytage, the owner of the Kirklees estate, to hold a service of blessing at Robin's graveside. This followed rumours of vampire infestation, reports of finger width perforations in the earth above the tomb (suggested as escape routes for the 'undead') and disturbing news of the discovery in the vicinity of mutilated and blood-drained animals. The request was denied and a great furore erupted among the local clergy. Naturally, refusal encouraged

Ecclesia Sanctum Graal – the Rt. Rev Sean Manchester, Britain's foremost vampire hunter. (Barbara Green)

yet more nefarious activities, culminating on the evening of 22nd April 1990 in a visit by Britain's foremost vampire hunter, the Right Reverend Sean Manchester, an associate of ISAIVLR – the International Society for the Advancement of Irreproducible Vampire and Lycanthropy Research. Accompanied by two assistants and bearing the paraphernalia of the vampirologist's and exorcist's craft, the clergyman entered the wood. One helper was so terrified that he immediately left the scene, only to pass the dismembered and blood-drained body of a goat that lay in his path. Reaching the grave, Manchester readied the crucifixes, holy water, garlic and candles and prepared to initiate the ancient rites. But the ceremonials were disrupted by an horrific screech. Three tense but uneventful hours elapsed until, faintly, a soft wailing echoed through the woods, building to a crescendo of tortured sound. Grabbing a candelabrum replete with five burning candles, the Reverend Manchester confronted the approaching noise, shouting 'Behold the Light!' The wailing ceased but was replaced by the human cries of the lacerated assistant, who had fallen into a patch of brambles. Sternly he reported witnessing a gruesome sight, the appearance of a hag with blood red eyes. There were no further confrontations that night, but before he left, the Reverend Manchester doused the grave in holy water and planted cloves of garlic all around.

Away from the grave, there have been other disturbing experiences. Like Roger Williams, Barbara Green has also witnessed strange phenomena in her home, and around three years ago, the Vicar of Brighouse, the Reverend John Flack, was called in to bless her property. There have also been mystifying happenings in the Three Nuns Inn, a hostelry standing on the site once occupied by the refuge of the homeless nuns of the sixteenth century. Some time ago, whilst the inn was in the process of refurbishment, workmen found a ram's head with the face of the devil, behind an old fireplace. The head was removed, with eerie consequences. One day, manager Richard Copeland reported feeling an icy hand on his shoulder. He turned to find no one there. He also described other strange occurrences. With nobody near, bar pumps turned themselves on and kitchen equipment switched itself on and off. 'I was mystified', said Richard. 'Then I was told of black magic links. I was informed of a tradition that anything found within the walls should be left there to keep the spirits happy.' The ram's head was duly put back and the inn returned to normality.

Such is some of the present mystery and controversy surrounding the area of the grave. It seems that the lack of any firm, empirical evidence upon which to base sound judgments, the inordinate lapse of time since the outlaw's death, and the welter of recent, some would say, fanciful and inventive stories proposing connections with sorcery, witchcraft and devils, all produce the climate for morbid escapism and sensational obfuscation. But dismissing all black distractions, surely there is only one way ahead for England's legendary hero.

The mysteries should be laid to rest in a highly formal and public ceremony of Christian exorcism and blessing, accompanied by atonement for past preoccupations with sinister forces. The site should be bequeathed to the nation, and it should be cleared of its melancholy shroud of trees, landscaped and planted and crowned with a suitable monument raised by public subscription. And, dismissing in advance all charges of romanticism or sentimentality, I say that the essential goodness of 'Robin' should be celebrated and allowed to shine forth, permitting lily-laden children to lay their wreaths and for the nation to say unashamedly that here indeed was an outlaw, the like of whom England will never see again.

2

THE SWALEDALE COVER-UP

The mystery of a murder at
Hollow Mill Cross, 1664

The Yorkshire moors hide many ancient secrets –
henges, strangely inscribed stones, obelisks, barrows
and bones, the arcane legacy of pagan worship, ritual
sacrifice and burial, and murder. Desolate and deserted,
these siren places inspire foul deeds and down the
centuries many grisly tales have been told of ambush,
brutal killings and interment in the black of night.

The infamous Hollow Mill Cross murder of 1664 is
certainly shrouded in mystery. Even today historians
wonder if this apparently isolated crime was linked with
government attempts to repeal the Triennial Act. Was
the death of John Smith in the spring of 1664 the
culmination of the successful purge of the Common-
wealth supporters of the so-called Kaber Rigg plot? We
shall never know.

The Triennial Act, passed in the sixteenth year of the
reign of Charles I, stipulated a three year maximum
period between one parliament and another. Wanting to
be rid of this legislation, Charles II instructed Gere, the
Sheriff of Yorkshire, to send incendiaries amongst the
people. In 1663, a group of ordinary men were duped

into planning an insurrection, having been told that the maximum parliamentary interval under the act had been exceeded, when, in fact, Parliament was in session. Rumours of a projected uprising in Yorkshire were rife. Justices and militiamen were sent to investigate but initially they failed to uncover a plot. However, incited by over-imaginative republican die-hards and agents provocateurs, an ineffectual uprising actually occurred. This was exploited to the full, Charles ordering his judges north with instructions to proceed with all possible severity. A supposed go-between for the plotters, a dales packman and pedlar by the name of John Atkinson, 'stockinger and Anabaptist', was arrested along with other suspects. In all, 26 men were tried and condemned to death and were hanged in Appleby. Just a day later, another travelling pedlar lost his life. Was the death of John Smith a residual settling of scores by a blood lusting judiciary . . . or was it murder?

Upper Swaledale is a vast expanse of heather and treeless summits riven by gills and ravines. It was first colonised by the Vikings, whose place-names ring out like clashing steel, the Norse hamlet of Keld being the last outpost of habitation on the road to Birkdale Common and the old border between Yorkshire and Westmorland. In the 17th century, an inscribed cross stood at the boundary of the two counties and it was this marker – the Hollow Mill Cross – that gave its name to this vile murder.

John Smith, the victim, was an itinerant buyer. He travelled the dales delivering wool and collecting finished woollen stockings and other garments from farmsteads and cottages along the way. According to several people who later gave testimony at the trial of the alleged murderer in York Castle, Smith spent the night of the 22nd March in Askrigg before crossing the moors and staying the next night in Swaledale at the house of a farmer, James Alderson. On the 24th March he set off for Kirkby Stephen market, with his two ponies heavily laden with merchandise and with a substantial sum of money in his wallet. He was never seen again.

There is some evidence that John Smith was bludgeoned to death near the Hollow Mill Cross. Everything else is rumour and speculation. Coming within only a few hours of the terrible happenings in Appleby, the incident sparked suggestions of a clandestine execution, the suspicions being fuelled by alleged sightings of two strangers labouring with a heavy bundle. Some time later a corpse was unearthed from the peat.

Many months after this, it was established that a Westmorland miner named Hutchinson knew something of the affair. According to local gossip, he was tormented by being aware of the identities of the assassins. He slept little, was visited by constant hallucinations and heard prompting voices in the night urging him to give evidence to implicate James Alderson and his two sons. The trial began before Sir Joseph Cradock and James Metcalfe at the York Assizes on the 11th December 1666.

On oath, Hutchinson recalled the events at Hollow Mill Cross. He was in the vicinity with a companion, Thomas Whiteheele. Both were searching for two horses lost upon the moor. Temporarily separated from his friend, Hutchinson heard an imploring cry, the single word 'Murder!' hanging on the wind. He also claimed he heard the sound of a single blow and the muffled conversation of two men. Tarrying awhile, he was approached by a riderless pony. Behind followed three men, one covered in gore. 'You have sure been fighting for you are all bloody,' said Hutchinson to the first man, who denied this and explained that the other two men were his father and a neighbour. All were pursuing a thief who had absconded with stolen goods after spending a night lodging at the father's farm. Hutchinson went on to give further detailed evidence.

After confronting the three men, Hutchinson walked on up to the place called Hollow Mill, where, looking down the gill he spied two additional figures, standing with their backs to him. Next to them on the ground was a nondescript object, resembling a bundle of clothes. Hutchinson wandered further still. He located Whiteheele and, gaining courage, together they returned towards the scene of the crime. From a distance they were observed by the three men, who were in the process of shifting a heavy load. Taking

A dark night at Hollow Mill Cross.

fright, these men jumped onto their horses and galloped off.

At the end of the following summer, Hutchinson attested further, that he and Whiteheele again visited the moor. The trial transcript records the following, 'coming nere to the place where they saw the two men bearing something, they began to looke aboute, and, in a waterhole, to their thinking, they saw the ribs of a man sticking in the bray, which when they had moved with a staff, fell into the water and swome... there was the corpse and head of a man with haire on it.'

31

As further proof of the Aldersons' guilt, Hutchinson described an alleged meeting twelve months later with George Alderson of Spenn House in Swaledale, 'hee said his father and his brother were gone out before after a poore fellow that was lodged there, and had stolen something, and hee followed them for feare they should get some harme, but, before hee came to them the deed was done. Hee said alsoe that his father was a very wicked man, and did not repent him of anything hee had done.' Hutchinson replied, 'Tell him from me hee shall heare from mee if I bee troubled in conscience or any other way.'

On this latter point, concluding his evidence, Hutchinson recounted a visitation at his house, '. . . there came a strange looking man with a sad coloured coat, and a poake tied about his shoulder and a staffe in his hand. ' Civilly, Hutchinson doffed his cap and asked the man's business. He said nothing, until the wife intervened and enquired of the stranger's religion. In the absence of a reply, Hutchinson proffered the idea that the man was a Quaker, whereupon the stranger snarled, 'The Quaker's religion is better than yours, for yours is a murthering religion. Hee that hath concealed murther is as bad as a murtherer.' In a final statement, Hutchinson explained that since the doorstep encounter, he had suffered much mental anguish and he had heard supernatural voices imploring him to tell the truth about the murder of John Smith.

One by one, subsequent witnesses undermined Hutchinson's testimony. Whiteheele flatly refuted everything his companion had said, strenuously denying ever being on the moor. Naturally, the Aldersons were interrogated at length and again they vehemently contradicted the accusations. And all Upper

Swaledale rallied to their defence. A petition dated 26th February 1666, signed by 106 prominent persons, including the curate of Muker and the vicar of Grinton, was presented to the court:

'Whereas one James Hutchinson of Hartley in Westmorland, who maliciously has gone about by his informacion to take away the lives, good name, fame, and reputacions of James Alderson, of Thwaite in Swaledale, and George and John his sonns, wee certifie that they have alwayes beene reputed and well knowne to be of good name, etc., not at all in any wise attainted, nor supposed to be of any leude or vicious behaviour, but honnest in all their dealings with all men, faithful subjects to his Majestye and his late Majestye of blessed memory, and lovers of all his Majestie's liege people. And we are fully persuaded that the informacion of the said Hutchinson and his complice is false, and by the instigation of that wicked one the enimie of mankind.'

Such was the incoherence and apparent inconsistency of Hutchinson's vastly contradicted evidence and the impact of the unequivocal support from the local community, that the jury found for acquittal. The Aldersons were released from custody and Hutchinson was dismissed. It is poignant to note that had the crime of perjury been on the statute books in the 17th century, this supposed liar might himself have dangled from a hangman's noose. As it was, he went home in disgrace.

Responsibility for the killing of John Smith was never finally determined. That, seemingly, was an end to the affair. But there is one last bizarre twist in the annals of the Hollow Mill Cross that must be told. Two years after his court appearance, James Alderson was returning home from a funeral when he was caught in a storm as he approached the county boundary. Here, according to local legend, he saw a ghost, presumed to be the murdered man. In a panic he pulled on the reins of his horse and the animal, already terrorised by the thunder and lightning, reared up and dashed its rider to death against the old stone cross. Some days later Alderson's widow found several parcels of stockings secreted under the floor of her cottage.

The discovery of those parcels brought into doubt the integrity of the whole judicial system. It was later claimed that in discrediting the evidence of Hutchinson, the honourable judges were acting upon government instructions in seeking the acquittal of a mercenary recruited to murder John Smith. If we accept this proposition we need to re-examine the evidence of the principal witness for the prosecution and to ask what

James Alderson returning home from a funeral.

possible motive other than to ease the burden of knowing could he have had for indicting Alderson, when there was no suggestion of enmity between the two men? And there is another burning question. Why was so much credence given to the trial petition? In jurisprudence, surely testimonies of previous good conduct should be irrelevant and should only be acknowledged in mitigation and in delivering verdicts, not in reaching conclusions of guilt? And, couched as it was, in sycophantic language most obsequious to the King, is not this document additionally suspect?

The mysteries of the Hollow Mill Cross murder have only deepened over the centuries. The cross itself has gone but its symbolism is forever embedded in a bloody chapter of Swaledale's history. Today, the border heights are little altered from the 17th century and the contemplative traveller may still stand here and admire some of the most starkly spectacular scenery in Yorkshire. And at the going down of the sun he may hear a plaintive piping, the bubbling, beseeching last post call of the curlew lamenting the deaths of John Smith and all those other unfortunates who have been murdered on the Yorkshire moors.

3

HOLY TRINITY

The mystery of a ghostly trio

Ancient York, according to a recent spectral census, is the supernatural capital of England. The old city is, to use a colourful Yorkshire expression, wick with ghosts. From a thousand years of history, dressed in everything from Roman togas to Victorian tail-coats, ghosts add a sinister yet alluring character to the snickets and snickelways of York, and no self respecting listed building or scheduled ancient monument is without its resident phantom. The magnificent Minster has its own distinctive spirits and dozens of other religious establishments also boast wraiths or poltergeists. All encounters with these ethereal beings have, however, been fleeting, insubstantial and sparsely recorded... apart from one... the subject of this intriguing tale.

Parts of Holy Trinity church in Micklegate are all that remain of a priory founded by St Oswald as a scion of the great French monastery of Marmoutier in 1089. According to one tradition, this building is said to have been the last redoubt of a courageous abbess who vainly resisted Henry VIII's attack on the monasteries. Resolute to the end, she openly defied the King's agents, declaring that they should only violate the holy domain over her dead body. The priory was entered and demolished and the lady was put to the sword, vowing with her last breath that she would haunt the scene of her execution until another sacred building was erected on the deconsecrated site. According to numerous early witnesses, she kept her word.

But there is another suggested provenance – a spectral trio said to be that of a devoted parent, a beloved little girl and her nurse. The father of the family had died and was buried at the east end of the church under or near the organ window. Weeks later, a virulent plague claimed the life of the child and, according to the medical practice of the age, she was laid to rest in quarantined ground outside the city walls. The distraught mother perished soon afterwards and was interred alongside her husband. Reunion must have been the aim of the ghostly tableau, the child being brought from its grave in the plague pit by her mother and a nurse for a sad rendezvous with her father.

'Whatever may have been the circumstances under which the ghosts commenced their promenade', wrote one observer in 1874, 'I would recommend those who have the chance to go to Holy Trinity church, York and see for themselves, though an audience of the apparition cannot always be assured. A ghost in broad daylight does no harm, frightens no one, and ought to interest everybody.'

For hundreds of years the ghostly manifestations, usually observed during services but in all weathers and at all times of the year, were reported by churchgoers and clergy alike, the avowed descriptions being notable for consistency and extent of detail. Witnesses in the 19th century agreed that three white clad figures traipsed across the east window with great animation. In earlier years the appearance of a male figure was recorded. The gait of the young mother, who was

Holy Trinity church, Micklegate.

attired in a beautiful gown, the folds of which hung 'like the drapes of a dress on a Greek vase' was variously described as a skipping or dancing movement. She preceded the nursemaid, a somewhat smaller and evidently older person, whose station was plainly evident from the passionate affection she displayed towards the child. The spectacle was, on occasions, momentary, but generally the action was prolonged. The testimony of a clergyman who witnessed a visitation in 1866 reads like the prologue of a tragic mime.

Centre stage, the lone mother beckons to the nurse, who enters with her charge. The two ladies bend over the child as if bemoaning its fate. The mother walks away, leaving the nurse, who waves a farewell. The scene is repeated, the gesticulations and entreaties becoming particularly agitated during the musical parts of the service. The whole pitiful performance is played out on the glass in much the same way 'as that of a magic lantern slide when seen on the exhibiting sheet'. The psychic screen – the window – is of gothic design and is divided into four multi-coloured quarters. Around its edge is a band of plain transparent glass, which affords an even clearer view of proceedings. Peculiarly, all the observations are made from the gallery where, traditionally, the Sunday school children sit. So often have they witnessed the familiar scene that they are becoming quite blasé about it, paying more attention to their lessons than the ghosts!

The spectres of Holy Trinity were regarded as a benign and fascinating oddity by most observers.

Successive incumbents, annoyed at the impious distractions, however, sought to dismiss them as chiaroscuropic tricks. Suggesting that several rectory garden trees were causing an optical illusion, one disgruntled rector ordered in the lumberjacks. But the offending trees were felled without effect. Hot under the collar, another clergyman wrote the following letter to the *York Herald*:

'I think the time has come when it is perhaps necessary for me to give a word of explanation in regard to this imaginary apparition. The fact is simply this: Anyone seated in the gallery of the church, which is at the west end, can see through the east window any person, or persons, walking in the vicarage garden. The wall at the east end of the church, below the east window, is too high to allow anyone in the body of the church to see either the garden or anyone in it. This fact explains at once the reason , how it is absolutely necessary for anyone to be in the gallery in order to see the 'ghost'. This is the real truth of the matter. What is seen is not a 'ghost'; it is not a 'reflection', but a living being, or beings, walking in the garden. Of course the east window being of stained glass and of a rather peculiar pattern, a distinct form is not always visible. And I may say that this simple explanation has been attested and verified over and over again both by myself and others. One argument of proof is all, I think, I need give. The Vicarage House was at one time empty for about 12 months, during which time the 'ghost' was neither seen nor heard of, and then it was let to a person with a large family; and on the very first Sunday after the family took possession of the premises, I was told by a simple minded youth that the ghost had returned, and five or six young ghosts with it. After what I have stated, I need hardly say that all the sensational matter in regard to vivid lights, mother, nurse, and child, extraordinary displays on Trinity Sunday etc, is as pure an invention as ever was fabricated by morbid imagination. And I will sincerely hope that the people of York will not take the advice of one of your voluminous correspondents, and will not go to church for the mere purpose of seeing this purely imaginative ghost. I trust that all who go will remember it is God's house, intended to be a house of prayer, and not a place for gratifying an idle curiosity.'

Such rationality and scolding appeared to sound the death knell for the Holy Trinity ghosts and, stirred to fill their inkpots, other correspondents wrote to a number of local newspapers, endorsing the rector's opinions and offering their own logical explanations for the visions. One lady suggested that a cottage window opposite the church was the real cause of the hauntings, explaining that the tenant of the cottage could cause the ghosts to appear and disappear at will by simply opening and shutting the casement and reflecting sunlight onto the church window. A second cleric joined the debate. His theory, a refinement of that suggested by his reverend colleague, proposed that refracted light transformed the images of passing pedestrians into spectral shapes. But there were dissenters. The swinging window proposition was quickly dismissed. Fixed glass would, it was argued, confine the thrown image to an immovable position on the window, it would be visible to the congregation seated in the main body of the

The ghostly vignette found by the author on the endpapers of Mr Cobb's prayer book. (York Reference Library)

church (this had never been the case), and it would not be seen in overcast weather. As for the more studied explanations offered by the clergymen, these were put to an acid test. 'One of my friends', attested an avid ghost watcher in an article published in the *Newcastle*

Daily Chronicle in 1874, 'with a companion, has watched outside on the wall, where he had full view of the whole place around during morning service. The ghost has been seen from the inside while outside nothing was visible.'

Since the sightings in the 1870s, the ghosts have vanished and parts of Holy Trinity have been rebuilt. The gallery has gone and the stained glass in the east window is modern, dating from the restoration by C.E. Kempe in 1905. In conclusion, none of the current congregation admit to observing anything untoward and that would appear to bring the curtain down on the ghostly trio. But I wonder?

Hundreds of intelligent, God-fearing people, some with a scientific bent, saw the ghosts, and the dismissive theory about the apparitions being reflections from visitors in the rectory garden was never proved. And anyone who examines the unaltered orientation and architecture of Holy Trinity's east window, will find nothing singular or unique to give rise to optical refractions or distortions. Similar situations exist in scores of churchyards throughout Yorkshire. So what happened to the ghosts? Were they finally reunited?

It was wholly fitting that my last source of material for this narrative was the Book of Common Prayer. By some strange quirk of fate, I came across a tiny volume in York Reference Library. Printed by Charles Bill in 1704, it has a note attached to its inside cover. This reads 'This volume formerly belonged to a well known solicitor of York, Mr J.W. Cobb.' The most curious thing in the volume is a vignette on the end paper representing the ghosts of Holy Trinity church. This very rare illustration is perhaps a contemporary record of an appearance of the ghosts . . .

4

A GHOST BY GASLIGHT

The mystery of the
Leeds Library, 1884-5

Ghosts...Pure fantasies, chimeras of moonlight and dark shadows, phantoms of firelight and fertile imaginations. So would claim the sceptics. In the absence of personal experience or irrefutable evidence, many people have forever dismissed the possibility of an ethereal world beyond our ken. In 1884, however, some close encounters with a wraith caused even sceptical lawyers to take note.

The distinguished setting for the visitation was the Leeds Library in Commercial Street, Leeds. Founded in 1786, this venerable institution for scholars and gentlemen survives to this day, retaining in aspic its mahoganied elegance and a collection of rare books and manuscripts that is the envy of private libraries throughout the world. Into this domain in 1857 came chief librarian Vincent Sternberg. A dedicated and an extremely conscientious lover of books, he was to occupy his post until his death in office in the early part of 1880. The same year brought a successor, but the jealous Sternberg was singularly reluctant to leave.

A Mr John Y.W. MacAlister was appointed to the

vacancy in May. An able and ambitious 24 year old who was to have a distinguished career, culminating in a knighthood in 1919, MacAlister immediately imposed his presence on the Leeds Library, developing and adapting its services to provide one of the finest bibliographic facilities of the day. It was the testimony of this intelligent, perspicacious and highly rational moderniser that was to lift the veil on the famous ghost, whose authenticity was subsequently attested by both the English and American Societies for Psychical Research.

The story began late one evening in the spring of 1884. For hours the library had been in total darkness save for the librarian's room on the first floor, where, in the glow of a guttering gas lamp, MacAlister worked on. Engrossed in his studies, he was oblivious to the lateness of the hour, but eventually he consulted his pocket watch. The time was 10.55 pm. He realised he had but a few minutes to rush from the building and to catch the last train to Harrogate, where he lived.

Picking up the lamp to light his way, he proceeded from his room along a connecting passageway. This led to a stairway down to the main book repository and the front door. He had stepped but a few strides when at the end of the corridor he saw a man's face. The following is MacAlister's account of the encounter.

'As my lamp illuminated this passage, I saw apparently at the further end of it a man's face. I instantly thought a thief had got into the library. This was by no means impossible and the probability of it had occurred to me before. I turned back into the room, put down the books, and took a revolver from the safe, and, holding the lamp cautiously behind me, I made my way along

A Strand Magazine (1908) reconstruction of MacAlister's encounter with the ghost of Vincent Sternberg.

the passage – which had a corner, behind which I thought the thief might be lying in wait – into the main room. Here, I saw no one, but the room was large and encumbered with bookcases. I called out loudly to the intruder to show himself several times, more with the hope of attracting a passing policeman than of drawing the intruder. Then I saw a face looking round one of the bookcases. I say looking round, but it had an odd appearance as if the body were in the bookcase, as the face came so closely to the edge and I could see no body. The face was pallid and hairless, and the orbits of the eyes were very deep. I advanced towards it, and as I did so I saw an old man with high shoulders seem to rotate out of the end of the bookcase, and with his back towards me and with a shuffling gait, walk rather quickly from the bookcase to the door of a small lavatory, which opened from the library and had no other access. I heard no noise. I followed the man at once into the lavatory and to my extreme surprise found no one there. I examined the window (about 14 ins. by 12 ins.), and found it closed and fastened. I opened it and looked out. It opened into a well, the bottom of which, 10 feet below was a skylight, and the top open to the sky some 20 feet above. It was in the middle of the building and no one could have dropped into it without smashing the glass nor climbed out of it without a ladder – but no one was there. Nor had there been anything like time for a man to get out of the window, as I followed the intruder instantly. Completely mystified, I even looked into the little cupboard under the fixed basin. There was nowhere hiding for a child, and I confess I began to experience for the first time what novelists describe as an 'eerie' feeling. I left the library, and found I had missed my train.'

When MacAlister eventually reached home in the early hours, he pondered on his adventures, resolving, during a sleepless night, to consult his colleagues on the visit of the mysterious stranger. 'Why that's old Sternberg!' declared the Reverend Charles Hargrove, a member of the library committee, upon hearing MacAlister's description next morning. Within minutes, the news of the ghostly visitation reverberated round the shelves and someone fished out a portrait of the former librarian (a photograph of a drawing). There was no mistake. Sternberg had a most distinctive physiognomy as a consequence of meddling with gunpowder. An explosion had removed his hair and eyebrows. MacAlister was startled. Staring up from the drawing was the face in the bookcase!

The year passed routinely without further incident, nothing more being heard from the unearthly visitor until the following winter when, one cold and dismal evening, two library assistants had an unnerving experience.

Alone on the premises, 20 year old senior assistant H. Rowlatt and junior library boy F.W. Pitts were working late in the Smoke Room, busy in the tasks of bookbinding and repair. A fire flickered in the grate as the pair worked studiously on until the embers died around 11 pm. It was time for home. Rowlatt described what happened next.

'All the lights in the place had been out for hours except those in the room we occupied. Before leaving, we turned out the gas. We then looked into the fireplace but not a spark was to be seen. The night was very dark, but being accustomed to the place, we carried no light. On reaching the bottom of the staircase, I happened to look up; when, to my surprise, the room which we had just left appeared to be lighted. I turned to my companion and pointed out the light, and sent him back to see what was wrong. He went at once and I stood looking through the open door, but I was not a little astounded to see that as soon as he got within a few yards of the room, the light went out quite suddenly. My companion from the position he was in at the moment, could not see the light go out, but on his reaching the door everything was in total darkness. He entered, however, and when he returned, reported that gas and fire were completely out. The light in the day time was got by means of a glass roof, there being no windows on the sides of the room, and the night in question was so dark that the moon shining through the roof was out of the question. Although I have often been in the same room till long after dark, both before and since, I have never seen anything unusual at any other time.'

Attached to this statement was a corroborative note from Pitts and an illustrative drawing.

Compared to MacAlister's detailed and dramatic account, the reports of the two assistants lacked substance and credibility. A third visitation, however, underlined the integrity of their claims and reinforced the growing realisation that the ghost of Vincent Sternberg was a palpable and a most persistent spirit.

At about 4 pm on the 1st April 1885, MacAlister and A.J. Edmunds, a classification assistant, were in the librarian's room. MacAlister was sitting, not unusually, at his table, ordinarily a utilitarian piece of furniture not given to strange behaviour. But on this occasion, it emitted a queer noise, likened by Edmunds to the vibration of a tuning fork. Seeking a logical explanation for the sound, Edmunds carefully examined the table, top, drawers, legs and all. Perplexed at finding no obvious sound source, he called in Rowlatt and all three colleagues discussed the mystery. Eventually, Edmunds' penny dropped. 'This has got something to do with old Sternberg!' he exclaimed.

The subsequent events were once more recorded for posterity, some time later Edmunds penning a note of events.

'I then remembered that Sternberg had died in the spring and that haunting phenomena were frequently associated with anniversaries. 'Cannot we discover' I askt (*sic*) 'the exact date of Sternberg's death?' 'Yes', said Rowlatt; 'old so and so down the street can tell us.' A messenger was despacht (*sic*) and returned with the news that Mr Sternberg had died on the first of April 1880, between four and five o'clock in the afternoon. I then put another question: 'Rowlatt, when Sternberg was alive, was there any sound that you were accustomed to hear in this library that at all resembled this?' 'Yes', he replied 'there was. Upon that spot on the table, whence this sound appears to proceed, there used to stand an old crackt (*sic*) gong, and when Sternberg wanted one of us boys he used to strike it and it sounded like what we hear.' Thus, upon the fifth anniversary, to the very hour, of the old man's death, a phantasmal bell reminded us of his presence.'

Certain that they had witnessed an act of communication from beyond the grave and impelled by a curiosity undiminished by the spookiness of the benighted library, Edmunds and Rowlatt and one other unnamed member of staff, met clandestinely later that day in the librarian's room. They seated themselves apprehensively at the culprit table and waited. Their vigil was soon rewarded. After a few moments, loud thumps were heard to emanate from the book-lined wall that separated the room from the lavatory where the hairless vision had disappeared a year previously. With great excitement, the trio proposed a method for communicating with the spirit, devising a simple code for spanning the great divide. Hasty experimentation soon revealed that a system of questioning followed by a series of responding knocks – three knocks for 'yes', two knocks for 'no' and one knock for 'doubtful' – would elicit the required information and an interrogation was begun, the knocker immediately revealing that he was indeed old Sternberg. And he was unhappy! Sternberg went on to admit that he would prefer extinction to the restless life of a ghost, an existence he blamed on agnostic attitudes and a dissolute life devoted to materialism. The interviewers concluded the seance by promising to pray for Sternberg's soul.

On the following morning, unable to contain his excitement, Edmunds confided in MacAlister, who referred the matter to the Reverend Hargrove. He listened to Edmunds' story with great interest and made immediate arrangements to hold a second seance, involving another prominent library committee member, George Hudson, and a lawyer. The gathering was solemnly convened and, as before, contact was established, the ethereal rappings and tappings being interspersed with chimes from the phantom gong. Hudson and the lawyer said little during the proceedings. Both were visibly shaken and dumbfounded, the lawyer later giving a warning to the library officials. 'Gentlemen', he said, 'this thing must never be known in Leeds. It must be hushed at once. There are women in this town who would never set foot in this library again. Mr MacAlister, you must instruct all your assistants to say no more about it.'

The edict of silence was dutifully obeyed but auditory phenomena, Sternberg's insistent call for attention, continued to be heard even by the library janitor. Inevitably, rumours of the ghost came to the ears of the library users and one day a bold young dandy accompanied by two titillated ladies of fashion, arrived hot foot on Sternberg's trail. They were disappointed. Sternberg was no peep show. His spirit went to ground never to be heard from again.

The ghost had visited an institution devoted to learning and research and it seemed wholly appropriate, therefore, that the diverse reports of manifestation should be subject to the most searching and scrupulous examination. This was carried out and rigorous interviews were held with all those witnesses involved. The conclusion? 'This was no legend of the Dark Ages, but the solemn testimony of ordinary men and women living in our own times.' The ghost of restless old Sternberg, it would seem, was real.

True to their promise, Rowlatt and Edmunds interceded with a God who, in life, Sternberg had consistently denied. Ever forgiving, perhaps it was He who finally closed the book on the ghost of Leeds Library?

5

TAXI!

The mystery of the fatal fare, 1951

Taxi driver Edwin Youll was instructed to pull over to the side of the road. He stopped and as he did so, a passenger levelled a handgun and fired. The .22 calibre bullet entered his head, lodging in his jaw and rendering him senseless. A brutal assault followed, both male passengers pulling the 14 stone driver from his cab by the feet and inflicting a merciless beating. Suffering from shock, multiple skull fractures and a massive brain haemorrhage, Edwin Youll soon died and his body was dragged some 15 yards from the road and dumped in a farm entrance. The killers escaped and despite a massive police hunt, they were never found.

Forty-three year old family man Edwin Youll was a popular member of the local community. A jovial and well-respected resident of North Ormesby near Middlesbrough, he was employed by a local firm – Horngold's Taxis. On that fateful Friday evening of 16th November 1951, he worked normally. According to the testimony of fellow taxi drivers, he picked up two men from the Middlesbrough railway station rank between 6.20 pm and 6.25 pm. Just ten minutes later his vehicle – notable for its eye-catching registration plate FUA 53 – was seen parked on the busy but unlit Ladgate Lane near the entrance to Newham Grange Farm and the

Youll's last fare was picked up from the railway station.

famous Blue Bell Inn. A few minutes later it had gone. Several hours elapsed before it was discovered abandoned four miles from the murder scene. Meanwhile, under the cover of darkness, a pool of blood on the roadway and Edwin Youll's mutilated body went unnoticed until 7.20 pm when the gruesome find was reported to the police.

Coordinated action involving the Middlesbrough, Newcastle, Durham County and the North Riding police forces was initiated and details were released to the newspapers. On the following day, the Saturday edition of the *Middlesbrough Evening Press* published an appeal for public assistance in tracing the killers. An article also appeared in the *Yorkshire Post* explaining how at first the assumption had been that Youll had been mown down by a hit and run driver. Within 24 hours, tentative investigations had alerted the police to the suspicious movements of an unidentified motorcycle and two cars – a Ford and a Standard. All three vehicles were observed at the scene of the crime around 6.35 pm. There were also the statements of a number of people who passed along Ladgate Lane in a car at the computed time of the murder. The consensus was that they had seen a man bending down beside the wheel of the taxi. Enquiries also produced two descriptions, one by a schoolgirl, of the suspect who had abandoned the taxi. He was said to be 'of stiffish build, medium height, dressed in a lightish or fawn coloured mackintosh or overcoat with a belt, and a trilby hat.' Subsequent reports, probably about the same person, gave more precise details, suggesting a height of between 5'8" and 5'10". Armed with this information, uniformed officers made door to door enquiries, paying specific attention to lodging houses and hostels. All port authorities were alerted to the need for the surveillance of returning crews and every opportunity was taken by the investigators to enlist public help, the Middlesbrough Chief Constable even addressing the crowd at the Middlesbrough/Derby football match in the relentless hunt for clues. During the first few hours of the investigation, the police made significant progress. Their satisfaction, however, evaporated in the light of the findings of the post-mortem.

It took an autopsy to discover that Edwin Youll had been shot. All the officers involved in the case had missed this vital fact and whilst the medical conclusion firmly established that the bullet wound had not been the cause of death, the character and scope of the investigation had been wrongly interpreted and misdirected. The police were keen to make amends.

A belated search for a firearm or spent ammunition was organised, using a metal detector. Nothing was found. The area was also combed for a possible murder weapon as the injuries on the body were consistent with blows from a heavy implement. Again, the search proved fruitless although dogged determination brought additional intelligence about the appearance of the suspects.

Reports came in corroborating the previous description of the first suspect but also giving new information about a second man. Observed at the railway station as he stepped into a taxi, he was vaguely described as dark suited and shorter in height than his accomplice. The mounting probability that the murderers of Edwin Youll had been casually seen by significant numbers of the public was at once both tantalising and frustrating. In the absence of more definitive information, police resources, it was acknowledged, were too thinly spread and it was decided to shorten the odds. A reward of £500 was offered seeking the vital lead that would reveal the identities of the killers. That reward has never been claimed.

Very few additional facts of substance were ever disclosed to the police in this perplexing case, but as that frantic weekend closed, a mysterious and abruptly curtailed note was found in the buffet at Waterloo Station in London. A bemused cleaner picked up an innocent looking scrap of paper. Instead of tossing it away, she read its chilling boast:

'Saki and me got clean away from that job. The driver has had it now. I held him down and Saki kicked the back of his head in. We dragged him into a hedge back and then drove the taxi to Middlesbro. It sure was a good idea doing the job near the Blue Bell because . . .'

Agonisingly, the concluding part of the sentence had been torn away. After discussing the matter with her workmates, the cleaner pocketed the note and went home, where she had further words with her husband. Shortly afterwards, he read about the murder in the newspaper and, assuming a connection, contacted the local police who in turn alerted their Middlesbrough colleagues. They were intrigued. Was the note the idle scribblings of an attention-seeking crank or a triumphant black confession?

The analysts who poured over every loop and squiggle of the handwritten note had cause to believe it was genuine. At the time of its discovery, news of the likelihood of two murder suspects had not yet reached the capital. Nor had the mention of the Blue Bell Inn. As for the assertion that the multiple skull fractures had been as a consequence of a frenzied kicking, this was conceded by the police medical experts as a distinct possibility. And there were more subtle hints. The abbreviated word 'Middlesbro' was in common local usage, and the reference to 'hedge back' – again a highly localised term – pointed to someone who at least was familiar with the vernacular of the North Riding. And what of the name 'Saki'? The police pursued this slimmest of clues with vigour, questioning numerous persons with variant names like Sackie and Sacky. All their investigations came to nought, despite a massive response from the public, who at one stage were submitting over 50 letters a day to the enquiry team.

In Middlesbrough, the murder generated a climate of fear and acute anxiety, especially within the female population and amongst the close knit fraternity of taxi drivers. There were clamourings for protection and, without foundation, wild rumours of additional murders. A woman was reputed to have had her throat cut. Another was alleged to have been strangled. It was little wonder that the hard-pressed police were anxious for an arrest. They widened their sphere of investigation and, acting on a tip-off, stormed aboard a departing ship in Hull. Another false trail! They increased the bounty for reliable information to £1,000 and they compared notes with other constabularies who had experienced similar attacks on taxi drivers. Nothing. Scores of files and hundreds of statements were assembled and closely scrutinised, and a vast bureaucratic mountain of ancillary paperwork was accumulated in pursuing the elusive breakthrough that would lead to an arrest.

Hopes rose with the opening of two new lines of

enquiry. An old gentleman and a Redcar insurance agent both recalled seeing two suspicious looking men on the Middlesbrough-Saltburn bus on the night of the murder. It was suggested that these men were responsible for stealing £8 from the conductress's fare box. And there was also the delayed testimony of a cyclist who alleged he had seen the taxi being driven back to Middlesbrough at around 7.10 pm. Travelling at excess speed, the vehicle had been particularly noticeable when it momentarily stopped at a crossing. The cyclist also remembered seeing the distinctive number plate – FUA 53. More importantly, he gave the best description yet of the two suspects. The passenger is said to have sported a Stetson over his light coloured hair and to have worn a raincoat. The driver was described as dark. He was dressed in a blue or dull coloured suit and, perhaps this latest snippet of seemingly trivial information authenticates the report beyond doubt, he incongruously carried a satin-lined raincoat over his arm. Fighting for his life, had Youll managed to wound one of his assailants . . . in the arm?

Like the identities of the killers, the motive for the murder of Edwin Youll is a mystery. As four pound notes were found on the victim, robbery can definitely be ruled out, as can a revenge or grudge killing, the police establishing beyond doubt that the mild mannered and good natured Youll had no enemies. This public spirited citizen had recently gone to the assistance of a blind man and, had he lived, he would have received an award on the 20th November during the Middlesbrough Accident Prevention Council Courtesy Week. With great pride and sorrow, the honour was accepted by his widow.

What are the other hypotheses? For me, the sequence

of events suggests that the murder was not premeditated. Surely, if this had been the case, the killers would have hijacked the taxi and instructed Youll to drive to a remote spot for his execution? And would there be any sense in attempting to shoot Youll dead, risking discovery, on an overridingly busy, albeit benighted, public highway, if the situation had not demanded his immediate silence? What dark intent had Youll uncovered? Guns were seldom used by criminals in 1951 unless in professional assassinations, so were the two men contract killers whose real assignment was at the Blue Bell Inn, and had they been thwarted by the suspicions and stubbornness of a taxi driver who, having spied a firearm, threatened to summon the police? And what of that note?

All is a farrago of unanswered questions and, so many years later, the trail has long run cold. If the killers are still alive, by now they will both be old men. But they might yet have cause for sleepless nights. The file on the murder of Edwin Youll remains open.

6

THE PHANTOM OF OLD SNYDALE

The mystery of the gory ghost, 1965

In the world of the occult, the connection between violent death and hauntings is well attested, numerous accounts of tormented souls having been recorded down the years. Some reports are highly fanciful, but others, affirmed by sober and well respected members of the public, make us all wonder about the existence of ghosts.

Supernatural detective work links the appearance in October 1965 of a phantom in the unlikely setting of Old Snydale, a small hamlet between Normanton and Featherstone in West Yorkshire, with the grisly murder of stablehand William Longthorne, 137 years earlier. The details of the killing and the subsequent experiences so many years later of several passersby, who chanced upon the site of the slaying, make for chilling reading.

The story began early on the cold morning of the 17th October 1828. Hailing from Barmby Moor near Pocklington, hard working 18 year old William Longthorne left his overnight halt in Wakefield. Seeking work in great heart, he set out on foot for Ferrybridge, a popular staging post for coaches plying the Great

North Road. Longthorne was accompanied on this his final journey by a companion, William Mosey, a dishevelled, shifty-eyed stranger dressed in dirty cotton trousers, a blue striped smock and a hairy cap. He was subsequently described by one witness as a low, broad-set, black-looking man. Mosey had cultivated the friendship of his intended victim the night before, his vile ambitions driven by the sure knowledge that Longthorne had secreted a considerable sum of money in his breeches.

Mosey distracted Longthorne in idle banter as they crossed Heath Common, but as the pair were nearing Dole Close in Old Snydale, he fingered the readied blade hidden deep in his pocket. Then he struck without warning, bowling over the stunned and perplexed Longthorne, who lay on the ground senseless. Mosey pounced and cut Longthorne's throat from ear to ear with a razor, severing the windpipe and carotid arteries, which immediately spewed blood. Stealing five shillings and a small bundle of clothes, Mosey dragged the critically wounded young man to a nearby beck, threw him into the water, and made a hasty escape. The cries were, it was reported later, heard by a stooping farmhand in a nearby field. He raised himself up to listen but hearing no more, went on with his work.

No stranger to bloody assaults, Mosey had wielded the butcher's knife before and he reckoned that Longthorne would quickly perish. But the cold water had a therapeutic effect. The flow of blood was temporarily staunched and a delirious Longthorne managed to crawl from the beckside to the back door of a nearby property, Alsop's House – now the Cross Keys inn.

Frantic tappings roused the occupants of the inn, who immediately summoned the local minister, the

Alsop's House — now the Cross Keys inn.

Reverend Hodgson of Normanton, together with a Dr Buchanan of Loscoe and a surgeon from Pontefract. Both doctors worked feverishly to sew up the gaping wound and eventually Longthorne recovered sufficiently to mumble weakly. But speech was excruciating. A slate and chalk were sent for and the ebbing Longthorne was encouraged to scratch out the name of his assailant. He scrawled the briefest details of his ordeal...but the identity of his attacker remained undiscovered. The police were called for and they began interviewing fellow travellers who had encountered Longthorne and Mosey along the way, their enquiries taking on a new urgency when Longthorne died.

An inquest, presided over by the coroner, Mr Thomas Lee, examined the facts of the vicious affray, the jury hearing the testimony of a lady who identified Longthorne and Mosey together on that fateful morning. They also listened to the evidence of the farmhand and that of a third witness, a man who had passed Dole Close shortly after the attack had taken place. He had noticed bloodstained grass on the verge but, seeing no further evidence of mischief, he had moved on. The medical experts presented their findings. Then the verdict. Guilty! William Mosey was indicted on a charge of wilful murder and the hunt was on!

Strenuous efforts were made to apprehend the felon but he was not found. Although posters proclaiming the crime of William Mosey were widely circulated, he remained at large. His disappearance was a mystery in itself but there were other bizarre aspects of the case. An inventory of Longthorne's belongings showed that he was far from being poor. The contents of his pockets, even minus five shillings, were not consistent with the rewards of a stablehand's trade.* The sovereign, the guinea note, the eight shillings in silver ... were they the proceeds from a night of sustained gambling? Had Mosey been cheated? Why else should he have purloined just five shillings when several months' wages lay beckoning? These enigmas surrounding the brutal slaying of William Longthorne are puzzle enough. What then will you make of the ghostly incidents reported in 1965 in the very month and at the very scene of his demise?

* In sifting through the West Yorkshire archives in search of the coroner's report, I chanced upon an indictment for one William Longthorn (no 'e') to appear before the 'next Quarter Sessions' on a charge of indebtedness 'to our Sovereign Lord the King in the sum of twenty pounds ...'

The first accounts of a supernatural presence came from a lady employed in the theatre. A Normanton resident, she had spent the evening in Doncaster and was driving home via Old Snydale. She recalled that as she approached a tight bend, immediately before the site of a former railway bridge, she was alarmed to see the figure of a man standing precariously in the middle of the road. Thinking he might hurry to safety, she carried on. At that moment, an instantaneous coldness pervaded her whole body. A collision was imminent. Surely the headlights of her car would warn the seemingly oblivious pedestrian? He did not flinch. The vehicle closed for impact and the terrified driver gripped the wheel ready to swerve. Then she saw his face and upper body, a morass of blood and strangely antiquated clothing twinkling in the headlights. Her heart pounding she managed to take avoiding action and raced by, bringing her car to an abrupt halt. In some trepidation she opened the door and, without leaving the safety of her seat, swung round, steadying her shaking body by anchoring one foot on the road. She peered towards the spot where the man had been standing. Nothing. She called. Silence. The creeping fear and numbness returned and, quivering with panic, she scrambled back into the car and drove off at speed. A trick of the night? A self-created chimera of starlight and shadows? I think not. Not many days elapsed before the apparition was reported again...by the same unfortunate lady.

What compelled a woman who had been scared rigid by an extraordinary experience to return to the scene of her encounter? An overriding curiosity certainly and, perhaps, a subliminal call to rendezvous that fear could not deflect. Just two weeks later she found herself approaching Old Snydale again . . . in the dark.

With headlights blazing, the lady negotiated the familiar bend and approached the site of the old bridge. She followed the stabs of light, every sense focused on the white line. Not there! She breathed easier for an instant. Then she saw him, nearer to the abutment this time, his back turned and his imploring arms outstretched as if supporting some great load. He turned, revealing his tortured face and bloodstained clothing and, at the last moment just before the car came broadside, he sprang in front of the wheels.

Given no time to react, and afforded only the briefest fraction of a second to brake or swerve to avoid a crash, the driver bore on, bathed in cold sweat and quaking in horror, bracing herself for impact. But instead of the sickening conflict of hurtling metal and flesh and bone, there was unimpeded progress and silence, the vehicle continuing on track as though passing through a mist. Finally convinced beyond doubt that she had really seen a ghost, the lady depressed the accelerator and roared away from the scene, not daring even to confront the rear view mirror. She vowed never to visit Old Snydale again.

Uncorroborated, the accounts of the mysterious happenings received only a modicum of publicity. Local residents were sceptical about the reports, dismissing the story of the phantom with a mixture of ridicule and fun. After all, was this not the season of Halloween? Over pints in the Cross Keys, the locals held ribald discussions about the appearance of their newly discovered celebrity. But the jocularity was soon dispelled. The guffaws had hardly subsided when one of the regular pub goers was accosted by a strange force.

Every weekday evening, as regular as clockwork, this

The winding road on the approach to Old Snydale.

person called at the inn on his way home from work. This pleasant routine had continued for years without incident until closing time one dark night in that same October. The curfew bell rang at 11 o'clock and the man made his way to his motorcycle to begin his journey home. He kick-started his machine, left the car park and headed towards Normanton, gathering speed. He saw nothing to disturb his mood of peaceful reverie. He heard no sound save the purr of his vehicle. He was completely unprepared for what happened next.

Suddenly, from behind, with the assuredness of a boa constrictor, a pair of arms encircled his waist. He turned instinctively, expecting to see a passenger, a daring prankster perhaps who had somehow managed to jump onto the pillion seat. He gaped in utter disbelief. The back suspension had, he noted, dipped considerably but the rear seat was empty.

The ghostly embrace was accompanied by a marked fall in temperature, and the biker recalls that he was enveloped in freezing vapour. This persisted for some time but disappeared simultaneously along with the clasping sensation as the cycle was slowed to negotiate a sharp bend. The man roared away in great excitement and pledged, like the lady before him, to steer well clear of Old Snydale. In the hamlet, talk in the Cross Keys took on an altogether more serious tone, especially after reports of a third weird encounter, this time involving a bus driver.

The two sole lady passengers on the last bus between Pontefract and Featherstone sat at the front of the single decker, contemplating their promised cocoa and slippers. Preoccupied with thoughts of ending his shift, the sleepy driver was likewise engaged until he noticed twin orbs of light approaching from the opposite direction in the vicinity of Old Snydale. Headlights? He thought not. The driver insisted that the illumination had a strange appearance never previously encountered in all his years on the road. As he tried to slow down, the bus and the lights converged, the twin beams melting into one brilliant circle of light with the distinct figure of a man clearly visible within its effulgent core.

The driver was not alone in witnessing the impending crash. Roused from her reflections, one lady screamed, warning of the immediate danger. It was too late. The bus ploughed into the unidentified obstruction with a resounding smash, the shockwave traversing the entire length of the vehicle. Bringing the bus to an emergency stop, the perplexed and, by this time, highly agitated driver jumped from his cab and prepared himself for the potential scene of carnage. But, mysteriously, the bus had escaped without a scratch and the road was completely clear. A gnawing coldness, the meteorological common denominator that had also characterised the two previous visitations, descended as the sphere of light departed over adjacent fields. All three witnesses of the incident, particularly the bus driver, were much distressed. Subsequently he had to seek psychiatric help and from that day forward he never drove professionally again.

The welter of evidence submitted by five independent witnesses, each supporting the controversial claims of haunting, caused great debate and local concern and it was resolved that the church authorities be summoned to exorcise the menace. Early in 1966, therefore, following prescribed ancient bell, book and candle rituals, the phantom was compelled to depart this realm. And as far as we know, he has never returned to trouble the people of Old Snydale.

There was, and there remains, some dispute about the provenance of the gory ghost. Several Snydale residents affirm that the spectre was the spirit of an unfortunate who committed suicide by jumping from the parapet of the old bridge. And yet there is some almost tangible evidence to provide a firm link with the murder of William Longthorne. The mutilated appearance of the ghost as described after the first reported sighting is consistent with the look of a man whose throat had been cut. All the sightings were in October – the month of Longthorne's death. Then there were the obvious localised connections. All the incidents happened in the neighbourhood of places associated with the murder and all involved fellow travellers on that infamous road. Longthorne had also passed that way. Was his spiritual presence a warning to beware of the lurking dangers of ambush, or was he seeking Mosey? We shall never know.

Longthorne was laid to rest in Normanton churchyard, his tombstone carved with an epitaph which concluded '. . . who was murdered most foul.' As for Mosey, he was eventually traced by the Wakefield Constables in September 1851. Longthorne might have had no cause to rise up if his murderer had been brought to book, but Mosey got off scot-free. Several important witnesses had by this time died and lawyers deemed there was insufficient evidence to secure a conviction. Somewhere, Mosey also lies buried. In the black of night I wonder if his soul walks abroad? Or for such as these are the gates of Hell forever locked tight?

7

A BARNSLEY BALLET

The mystery of the dancing stick, 1965

Reports of psychic phenomena are legion. Most accounts have a common context and setting – a person alone in ancient surroundings with twilight shadows and mists heightening the will-o-the-wisp nature that is the hallmark of the ghost and the poltergeist. It follows that psychic happenings in broad daylight are rare and that ghostly manifestations in the presence of dozens of people are even rarer still. So what will you make of the unique ethereal conjuring tricks actually captured on film in Barnsley in December 1965?

At the end of a week that brought blizzard chaos to Barnsley, 14 year old Michael Collindridge of the Cranberry Hotel in Dodworth Road was tucked up in bed. Suffering from a bout of tonsillitis, he had been prescribed physic, lashings of fruit and, to relieve the tedium, numerous back numbers of the *Dandy* and *Beano*. Transferred by his mum Dorothy from his own bedroom to the warmer quarters of his grandmother, the hotel licensee, Mrs Sarah Shepherd, Michael stoically settled down to yet another day of female fussing and

The Cranberry Hotel in Dodworth Road.

pawing, little knowing that the fun was about to start.

Twelve years before, Michael's aunt, Mrs Annie Wooffinden of Pogmoor, broke her leg. Her hobbling was assisted by a Malacca-cane stick, a well-worn implement that ultimately passed into the Collindridge household where it was used as a prod for opening windows. On the day of Michael's billeting, the stick was retrieved from its usual position on the floor and hung on the back of his bed, its newly elevated status causing an extraordinary stir.

Inanimate objects only take wing in cartoons and in fairy stories and this was no *Looney Tunes* nor was it a screen test for the *Sorcerer's Apprentice*. This was 'ee by gum Barnsley' in bleak December... So what was happening?

'The stick went mad', explained Dorothy Collindridge. 'It danced about on the bed head as if it had come to life and it scared us all stiff.' Michael was most perplexed. Thinking he had overdosed on comic strips, he rubbed his eyes in amazement as his grandmother rushed out of the room to telephone the brewery.

'I thought they would think I was going round the bend when I rang them', said Mrs Shepherd. 'But after I had explained it all, they decided to send an official to have a look. He was astounded when he saw the stick moving on its own. We decided to ask other people to witness the sight and Councillor Gordon Jepson came along to see it.'

A fusion of brass tacks and brazenness, the Yorkshire councillor is a force majeure in uncovering wheezes. Jepson was a captain of his clan and immediately upon visiting the sick room he set about investigating the outlandish claims of a dancing stick.

He smelt a mechanical rat and asked Michael to put his hands on the top of the bed. The lad obliged but the stick continued to hover. The councillor next dropped to his knees and looked under the mattress. No strings! Flummoxed, he checked the floor and the walls but still found nothing to explain the levitation.

'I didn't believe it at first', he admitted 'But I had to believe it when I saw it, although I am still baffled by it.'

By this time, Michael's bedroom and the downstairs bar had become a regular media mecca and till receipts were noticeably up, the local newspaper slyly remarking, 'The spirits at the Cranberry Hotel seem very well disposed and obliging to all and sundry.'

In the wake of councillor Jepson came dozens of pub regulars, several masters from Barnsley Holgate

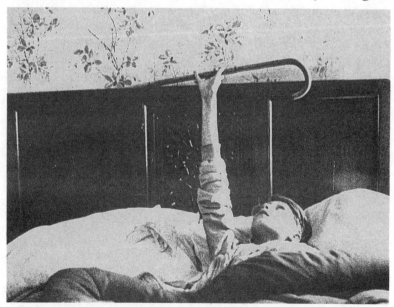

Michael Collindridge and his performing stick. (Michael Shepherd)

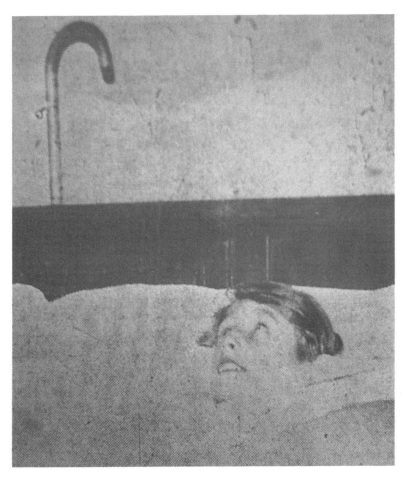

Michael watches the stick go through its paces. (Barnsley Chronicle)

Grammar School, where Michael was a fourth-form pupil, and two magicians. Paul Denver, a professional from Rhyl, was accompanied by Alexandre Forbes, an amateur conjurer from Barnsley. Like the councillor, they too carried out a thorough examination of the bed

75

and room and, like Jepson, they left bewildered.

Denver commented, 'The only way this could be done as a conjuring trick would be by radio control; and I have found no evidence of the necessary equipment in this room.' And although he didn't visit Barnsley, David Nixon, the famous television magician, also gave an opinion, 'If the boy is controlling this stick as part of a conjuring trick, he has a great future ahead of him. I have done levitation tricks, but I doubt if I could fool the number of people who have seen this at such close range.'

Despite these dismissals of trickery, scepticism arose when it was discovered that Michael was a keen amateur conjuror and had attended meetings of the Barnsley Circle of Magicians. When pressed on the matter, he strenuously denied any subterfuge, saying, 'I do conjuring tricks for children's parties and I am interested in conjuring. I only wish I could work a trick like this.' Michael went on to explain that, after overcoming his initial fears, he began treating the stick as a performing dog. 'I got used to it after a while and began trying to make it do things. I asked it to jump and it left the bed and went into the air and landed back on the bed.' Encouraged, he carried out another experiment. He asked the stick questions, receiving answers in the form of coded knocks, and he even taught it to tap out the rhythm of popular songs, including *Jingle Bells*, *Auld Lang Syne* and *Rule Britannia*. It certainly beat doses of Fennings Fever Cure and Desperate Dan!

But Dorothy Collindridge was worried. The antics of the stick were weird and unnatural and it was unceremoniously banished to the landing. Next morning, however, it was found stuck to the bedroom door as if with glue.

Press reports about the magic stick continued to appear and more journalists and photographers descended on the Cranberry Hotel. A reporter from *The People* Sunday newspaper wrote the following, 'There was no metal connection through which the stick could be manipulated. I examined it carefully. It was a very light stick and worn with years of use. There is nothing to indicate what made it perform. I don't believe it, but I saw it happen.' And the *Sheffield Morning Telegraph* published genuine photographs of the stick in unaided

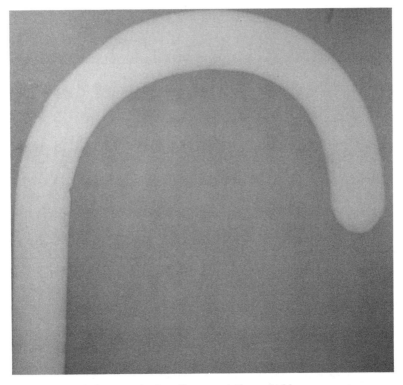

An X-ray of the cane's handle revealed no hidden magnets.

77

flight. It was indeed hot news and yet more people clamoured at Michael's bedroom door. Some visitors were extremely sceptical, one accusing magician suggesting a charade based on the hidden use of magnets acting upon metal fittings cleverly concealed inside the stick. This hypothesis was incontrovertibly disproved by a visit to the X-ray department of the local hospital. Like Pinocchio's nose, the stick was made of solid wood.

One Sunday evening, two reporters and two other visitors obtained permission from Mrs Collindridge to attend the bedside circus. At 8 pm, accompanied by Mrs Shepherd, they waited expectantly for the show to begin. Nothing happened. While he was waiting, one reporter took the opportunity to scrutinise the stick and everything in the room. He had just concluded his inspection when the action began. The following detailed report was published the next day:

'There was nothing as far as I could see which might make the stick move. I handled the stick and searched it from top to bottom to see if it had been tampered with in any way, but the only marks I could find were those made by constant use. The bed is about four or five inches away from the wall and it has a perfectly normal bed head. The only 'foreign body' behind the bed was an electric cable leading to Michael's bedside. The wall is plainly papered and did not appear to have been tampered with in any way which might have made it possible to conceal any machinery. Satisfied that there was nothing mechanical which could make the stick move, I questioned Michael and his grandmother about it. Both were extremely sincere and I cannot believe that either of them would attempt to make up a story such as they told me.

'Michael seemed to be enjoying showing off the stick to visitors, but in my opinion if there had been any trickery on his part he would have made the stick perform for every single visitor, whereas many people stayed in the room for some time without seeing a performance. Mrs Shepherd told us how a photographer had tried to take photographs but was unsuccessful. He was asked to take his camera outside and as soon as he did so the stick began dancing. She told how he crept slowly out of the room and returned equally slowly with his camera only to see the stick drop to its resting place and remain there unmoving.

'"The same thing happened when certain other people have been in the room", she told me. "I don't know why this is, but the stick has started dancing when they have left and always stops when they return."

'This appeared to be the case while the four of us were in the room, so to find if any one of us was the "bad influence", we left the room one at a time but still the stick remained motionless. Eventually two of the visitors left, leaving myself and another reporter in the room. We were determined to see for ourselves even if it meant staying there for an hour, and we remained talking to Michael and Mrs Shepherd.

'We had almost given up hope and had nearly forgotten that the stick was there when suddenly two raps drew our attention to the bed head. There we saw the stick slither along the head of the bed completely from one side to the other. Then without any signal from anyone it began to tap out the rhythm of "Jingle Bells". By raising itself about an inch above the bed and returning, the tapping sound was produced. The rhythm was at apparently correct tempo and even had we not been told the tune, we could have recognised it. We stood speechless for a while, not believing our eyes and ears but when we recovered we asked Michael to put the stick through its paces.

'He knocked three times on the bed head and the stick replied three times. We asked him to ask the stick if there would be a war within the next 12 months and for the stick to answer one knock for "Yes" and two knocks for "No". The stick replied with two knocks – much to our relief. Michael then asked the stick to rise from the bed head. At first it did not move but after some pleading from him it rose slowly to about 12 inches above the bed, but the bottom of the stick was never visible. Michael then asked the stick to jump and it rose sharply from the bed to a distance of about 12 inches. When it dropped it failed to hook itself over the bed and fell down behind. Michael asked: "Are you alright?" but there was no response. He asked: "Are you stuck?" at which the stick rattled itself against the leg of the bed.

'While the stick was in this position I leaned back from my chair and peered under the bed. I could see the whole stick plainly moving with nothing else near it. The stick did not rise back to the bed, although Michael says that it usually does, although sometimes coming up the wrong way.

'We returned the stick to the bed and awaited further antics but none came. Michael asked: "Are you alright?" but the stick remained motionless. He picked up the stick and examined it. Returning it he said:

"You are alright, you're not hurt", but the stick did not move. He then asked: "You don't think I would tell fibs do you?" and to our amazement the crook of the stick moved from side to side as if shaking its head to say "No". We watched for another minute or so as the stick pranced about on the bed head. Then a young lady came up to see the stick and no sooner had she entered the door and seen it move once, than it stopped and refused to move.

'I do not believe in ghosts, but I left the room convinced that no human power could have been responsible for moving the stick. I have always been of the firm belief that there must be a reasonable explanation for everything which happens, but as yet, I have not heard one for this.'

Although the pronouncements of the Society for Psychical Research gave the events credibility, one representative noted 'disturbances of the type described here occur at a certain stage of the development of an adolescent. Some parapsychologists believe that the manifestations can be the effect of psychokinesis, or the influence of mind over matter . . .'

The phenomenon of the dancing stick was explained by some people as a very clever hoax. All I can say on the subject is, where was the motive? Such was the degree of sophistication in this unparalleled exposition of the conjuror's craft that Mrs Shepherd could have charged a substantial entry fee to the Cranberry Hotel and Michael Collindridge could have gone on to become a considerable star. So was it a poltergeist? And if it was, why did it manifest itself through a length of wood in an ordinary public house with no history of psychic activity?

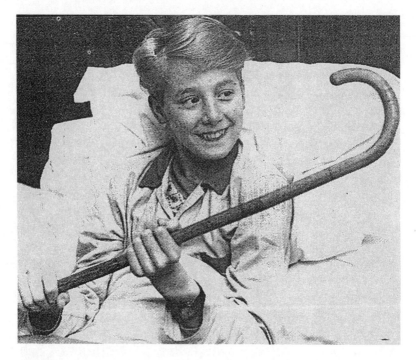

The bright-eyed teenager was asked to return to bed after his illness was over to pose for further press photographs. (Michael Shepherd)

Thirty years on, I researched this story principally by examining contemporary accounts and newspaper articles. And I did something else. On the off-chance that Michael Collindridge might still be in the neighbourhood, I consulted the Barnsley telephone directory and, finding the number and address I sought, I despatched a letter asking for information. A *Malcolm* Collindridge wrote back!

There are two final twists in this tale. In his reply, this gentleman recounted the bizarre experiences of his daughter, Janet, who in 1976 worked at the Mount Pleasant Hotel near Bawtry.

A 15 year old apprentice chef, Janet worked long hours in the kitchen, only finishing work near midnight. To avoid late night journeys home, Janet's employer arranged for her to sleep in the women's quarters in an old converted barn near the hotel. One morning, after completing her shift, Janet returned to her room to lie down, but upon entering the building, 'she saw an old lady dressed in black, sweeping the corridor with an old brush made of twigs. She said hello to her and continued on her way.'

Puzzled by the incident, Janet discussed the matter with other staff. They all denied knowing anything about the strange visitor. Some time later a new girl starter walked into the dormitory and screamed, watching in horror as the old lady disappeared through a wall. There is a postscript at the foot of Mr Collindridge's letter: 'PS. Janet worked there for about 15 years and her employer bought all the staff a book each. Yes, you've guessed it . . . a BIBLE.'

Was it a sheer coincidence that two teenage Collindridges in successive decades had paranormal experiences, and can there be any other members of the family out there with similar tales to tell?

I mentioned two twists in the tale, and the last is an even more extraordinary turn of events than the first. Well, completely out of the blue, I received a telephone call from a Mr Shepherd of Dringhouses in York. Apparently, in 1965 he had been confined to bed with tonsillitis and had since changed his surname! I visited Michael and heard at first hand about the authentic mystery of the dancing cane, an implement he still retains, a common or garden stick that has been quiescent ever since.

8

A MISCHIEVOUS SPIRIT

The mystery of the Black
Monk, 1966

According to experts, poltergeists are defined as the practical jokers of the underworld. Worldwide studies have revealed them to be capable of extraordinary acts of impishness, individual phantoms each having their own singular repertoires. Specialities embrace puddle forming, missile throwing, furniture levitation and dematerialisation of household objects, all coupled with a predisposition for creating chaos and fear and the maximum amount of noise. Individually, each party piece is frightening and tiresome in the extreme, but collectively, when manifest in the antics of uniquely busy sprites like the one who takes centre stage in this mystery, they are terrifying.

Dubbed the 'Black Monk of Pontefract', in reference to a reprobate friar who was hanged for rape at the time of Henry VIII, but more prosaically referred to by the long-suffering subjects of his attentions as 'Mr Nobody' or 'Fred', the poltergeist first came to Pontefract in August 1966. His choice of abode was the unassuming family home of Jean and Joe Pritchard of 30, East Drive. An unannounced visitor, he was to stay three years.

Holidaying in Devon, Mr and Mrs Pritchard and their daughter Diane were blithely unaware of the unfolding drama back home, where Mrs Pritchard's mother, Sarah Scholes, had been left to supervise 15 year old grandson Phillip. Taking advantage of a balmy Thursday morning, the pair relaxed. Phillip read a book in the garden. His grandmother sat indoors knitting a cardigan. Suddenly the lady was aware of a distinct chill. Then, although there had been no wind, the door slammed shut and all the windows began to rattle. Phillip entered the house. 'Is there a wind getting up?' asked Sarah. 'No. It's quite

Did the Black Monk know this entrance? Pontefract has a wealth of monastic history – most brothers lived communally but others lived in solitary retreats like the subterranean Hermitage, located below modern day Southgate.

calm out there.' Unconcerned, Phillip next went into the kitchen to make hot drinks. He returned ten minutes later with the teacups shaking.

With eyes only for her needles, Sarah was completely unaware of the mist of white powder descending from above. Dusted all over her, she looked up, spied Phillip through the haze and said accusingly, 'What have you been up to?' 'Nothing', said the stupified Phillip, 'I've been in the kitchen all the time. What is it?'

Phillip had great cause to be agitated. This was no simple shower of plaster. The ceiling had only recently been papered and, inexplicably, the fall of powder began neatly some feet below the top of the room. A no-nonsense Yorkshire woman, Sarah looked for a logical explanation for the dust. Finding none, she left the house and sought the opinion of her other daughter, who lived nearby. When the ladies returned, the powder was still falling and by this time it had formed a white veil over the entire contents of the room. A practical chip off the old block, the daughter readily assessed the situation and prescribed a solution. Fetch a cloth!

But there was a distraction in the kitchen. 'Are you sure you haven't had an accident?' shouted the daughter as she skidded on a substantial pool of water. 'I'm not senile yet', was the frosty reply. The daughter began mopping. She mopped again and again, but the water kept coming with the regularity of the buckets in the *Sorcerer's Apprentice*. Surely there was a leak underneath the linoleum? Peeling back the corner, she discovered that the floor was bone dry. Enter another neighbour, a lady who had heard the commotion through the party wall and decided to help. Taking charge of proceedings, she turned off the stop-cock. This made no difference so

The chilling outline of a skeleton holding a dart in its right hand, incised into the rock wall of the Hermitage.

the Water Board were summoned. A pimply faced youth dragging a box of spanners arrived within the hour.

The fall of powder had ceased by the time the plumber arrived but the seepage of water continued. The young man scratched his head, examined the floor, rodded the pipes and gave his verdict. Condensation! He left and one hour later the pools dried up. Dusted and dried, the house returned to normality...for a few hours.

Around 7 o'clock Sarah was watching television, until the programme was interrupted by an ejaculation. 'It's happening again grandma!' shouted Phillip, who was spellbound by an altogether more compelling viewing in the kitchen. 'Come here!' Speechless, he pointed. The work surfaces at the side of the sink were covered in sugar and tea leaves and the bemused pair looked on as

The Pritchards' family home in Pontefract.

a plunger on a tea dispenser went automatically in and out, spitting out more tea until the canister was empty. 'Stop it!' implored Sarah. 'I can't', replied Phillip. 'It's doing it on its own!'

From the hallway came a violent crash. Logic suggested an intruder. Sarah and Phillip gingerly opened the door and instantly the light went on. Nothing there! But what was that on the stair? A plant plucked from its pot. Its container was on the landing. Again the desperate desire for explanation but again disturbance by yet another discordant sound. They rushed once more to the kitchen to witness convulsions of the crockery cupboard. Phillip pulled open the door. The vibrations stopped but were replaced by banging somewhere else in the house. Eventually, the disturbances petered out and, with not a little amount of courage in the circumstances, Sarah and Phillip prepared to go to bed. But sleep would be a long time coming.

Phillip had already retired but without his goodnight kiss. An ever determined lady, grandma was insistent that her routine would not be broken. She entered her grandson's room and sat on his bed. He peered over her shoulder, riveted in disbelief, as his wardrobe performed a drunken dance. Even Yorkshire matriarchs baulk at such strange sights. 'Phillip, get dressed quick', she ordered. 'We're going.' A short time later, the relieved pair were ensconced in spare beds in a house nearby. The neighbours, Mr and Mrs Kelly, however, far from being dismissive of the almost unbelievable descriptions of what was by this time firmly acknowledged by Sarah and Phillip as a haunting, were intrigued. There was, they reasoned, a rational explanation. Criminal mischief was afoot. It was a case for the police.

A trio of bobbies arrived and began a minute search of No 30, East Drive. They found no signs of a break-in, nor any evidence of misdemeanour, and returned to the station. But the summoning neighbour was still not satisfied. He discussed the day's events with his wife well beyond midnight and, despite the lateness of the hour, they decided to consult a local sage, Mr O'Donald, a self-professed authority on ghosts. This night-owlish gentleman obliged. Escorted over the threshold of No 30, he was met with a rush of cold air. He sat down alongside the Kellys, the trio expectantly continuing their vigil, without incident, for well over an hour. A bored Mr O'Donald yawned. 'They do funny things, these poltergeists', he said, as he rose to leave. 'They're fond of tearing up photographs, I believe.' The Kellys followed him into the street and were preparing to lock up when they heard a crash. They rushed back into the house and there, lying on the lounge carpet, alongside two upturned paintings and amidst a sprinkling of broken glass, was a wedding portrait. This photograph of Jean and Joe Pritchard had been slashed with a knife.

For two years after this, the Pritchard household was undisturbed, but in 1968, as the family gathered for the August bank holiday and began discussing the by now famous haunting, Jean Pritchard had her first encounter with 'Fred'.

Jean was seasonally occupied in decorating Diane's bedroom. Intent on her painting, she was only mildly annoyed by the sight of a counterpane found incongruously dumped on the stairs. She replaced the covering and went on with her work, only to be distracted minutes later by a loud thud and the discovery of several upturned plant pots and a second

91

counterpane lying in the hall. Sarah read the ominous signs and lamented, 'I told you. It's starting again.'

Order was restored and the family retired uneasily to bed. Jean found the temperature oppressive and got up, feeling a pervasive and contradictory chill as she reached the landing. Trembling, she squinted through the gloom and detected a slight movement on the floor. A mouse? Pigs might fly! Jean switched on the light and a paint brush sped past her nose, closely followed by a self-propelled paste bucket that ricocheted off the wall and sent its contents flying. Back on the floor, the rodent metamorphosed into a demented cobra, in reality a roll of wallpaper dancing and swaying to some arcane charmer's tune. Bravely, Jean tried to grab the roll, but it evaded her grasp and floated gently to the floor. More frightening scenes followed. A carpet sweeper was raised up and brandished like a club. Jean fell to the floor and attempted to cry for help. She was struck mute for some seconds but managed to scramble away on all fours to the safety of the bedroom . . . Bang! A roll of wallpaper hit the door and Jean screamed, waking her husband and the two children.

Congregating on the landing, all four Pritchards became the targets of a veritable knife throwing act, paint brushes and other decorating implements whizzing past their heads. Diane was repeatedly hit. 'Don't stand there!' shouted her concerned father. Diane pondered for a brief moment and wonderingly said 'It didn't hurt.' The assault abruptly switched to Diane's bedroom where, in full view of Phillip, the window pelmet was ripped from the wall and flung through the open casement onto the path below. Angrily, Joe Pritchard slammed his daughter's bedroom door shut. There was a reciprocal thump from inside the room as Diane was consoled and led away to the comparative safety of her parents' bed.

For the next nine months, the Pritchards, inspired by the imperturbability and sheer stubbornness of grandma Sarah and her daughter, refused to be cowed by their ever attentive lodger. His daily visits became rather routine, even his regular conjuring tricks with levitating ornaments becoming somewhat unimpressive to his long suffering audience. His attentions were certainly tiresome and the family determined to turf him out . . . with the help of bell, book and candle.

Poltergeists, it would seem, are not impressed with chants and holy water. Experts in the mysteries of the paranormal claim that such spirits are impervious to the rituals of exorcism. Nobody imparted this stark fact to the Reverend Davy, who was invited to No 30 to perform the eviction. His visit was an unmitigated disaster. He spent an uneventful one and a half hours in the house before anything happened. Anxious to get back to the vicarage, he looked at his watch. Jean Pritchard was embarrassed and said 'I'm sorry we've dragged you all this way for nothing.' As she uttered the words, there was a series of loud thumps. A brass candlestick fell from the mantlepiece onto the floor. 'Subsidence', concluded the minister, almost choking on his words as the twin stick floated before his very eyes.

'Do you think that's subsidence?' asked Jean pointedly. The vicar's conversion was almost complete, a cacophonous tinkling from the next room and the sight of the entire contents of the crockery cabinet strewn over the carpet, finally convincing him that 'Fred' was all too real. 'There is something evil in this house', he said, 'I should think of moving.' With that he left. Had he stayed, he would have been in no doubt that Old Horny had indeed come from his lair, for the curtain was shortly to rise on the most diabolical act yet.

As Diane was on her way to bed, the lights went out and she was aware of an instantaneous coldness. A faint glow from a street lamp filtered through the glass in the door, allowing her to discern something moving in the hall. She blinked and her pulse raced as she noticed a huge, glowering shadow creeping towards her. The heavy oaken hall stand rose up, it too floating in her direction. In panic she stepped back and tripped on the stairs, the animated hall stand and a sewing machine that had stood on its surface, pinning her down as she fell. She struggled, too breathless to call for help, panting in dread and desperation to escape. She pushed with all her strength but was held fast. The lights went on and her frantic parents came running, tugging and pushing at the malevolent load that threatened to crush the life out of their daughter, who begged for release. Despite all the desperate clawing, the hall stand and the sewing machine held firm. But there was something even stranger. The near hysterical Diane was slowly placated by the reassuring words of her mother and by the increasingly obvious realisation that she was in no pain or discomfort. Despite the inordinate weight on her chest, she could breathe quite easily and she was persuaded to relax. She went limp and the hall stand and the sewing machine were lifted away without effort. Diane was, incredibly, no worse for her experiences, which in ordinary circumstances would almost certainly have resulted in fractured ribs or worse. She had no bruising and the thought that the ghostly perpetrator of the attack meant her no serious harm, eased her fears.

She was led off to her room, hoping that her ordeal was over. It was not.

Diane crawled into bed and turned off the light – a trigger for more prankishness. Her bed clothes were whipped away and tossed in the corner of the room. The attention seeking 'Fred' had a further surprise. He flipped over the mattress, catapulting Diane onto the floor. Heroically, she re-assembled her bed and once more prepared for sleep, only to find herself tossed into the air. Twice more during that sleepless night Diane became a trampolinist, landing each time with a thud. The molestation finally ceased but Diane lay awake all night.

Over the succeeding weeks, the obviously bored 'Fred' displayed both destructive and placid streaks. He smashed a grandmother clock and caused a sweet perfume to percolate throughout the house. He was also responsible for a drumming noise that could be heard over a wide area. Such newsworthy eccentricities naturally attracted the attention of the press and in September 1968 both the *Yorkshire Evening Post* and the *Pontefract and Castleford Express* ran exciting stories about the celebrity 'Fred'. He became a local tourist attraction! Bus drivers pointed out the 'haunted house' to their passengers and miners on their way to work would stop and listen for the 'phantom drummer'. Even knots of sightseers anxious to make his acquaintance would camp out opposite the house.

'Fred' obliged his public with more bizarre performances. On one occasion, when Jean was entertaining a friend to tea, the lights went out – his customary calling card. After the power was restored, it was found that something with enormous teeth had taken a bite out of a chicken sandwich. A little later, Jean's sceptical aunt had milk poured over her head from a hovering jug and she was entertained to further delights, including a performance by a line of dancing sausages. She blamed this on the kids! 'You've got the Devil in this house', she said at the end of her visit, vowing not to return, even for £20,000. A third, even more astounding incident, involved a number of eggs. One floated into the lounge and exploded, bathing the air with a delicious scent. Determined to thwart her annoyer and safeguard her omelettes, Jean retrieved the remaining eggs from the kitchen and placed them in a wooden box, upon which she sat defiantly. But her eggs kept materialising and bursting in the air until the box was empty.

After months of constant annoyance and disruption, the Pritchards were, predictably, even keener to evict their lodger. The Church of England had been singularly unhelpful in serving 'Fred's' marching orders, so they turned to the Church of Rome. A priest recommended that holy water be liberally sprinkled throughout the house. This was done one evening, with only adverse effects. Immune to such ceremonials, 'Fred' demonstrated his wrath by, appropriately, pouring water from the ceilings. And, incited by the efforts to evict him, he created further havoc, displaying his full range of talents.

By the next morning, the entire household was staggering around, sleepless and bog-eyed.

Worse was to follow. While Diane was standing by the kitchen fireplace, combing her hair, without warning a drawer slid out of a table, shot across the room and smacked her from behind. A more sinister missile hit her next. A mantlepiece crucifix leapt on her back and stuck fast. The terrified Diane could not prise it off. 'Get it off me', she pleaded with her mother. Both tugged but the crucifix stuck like a limpet. Shaking violently, Diane ran into the hall, convinced that this time the poltergeist intended injury. She heard something fall. The sign was baleful. The figure of Jesus was detached from its mounting and hit the floor and she ran on, frantically shaking herself free of the cross as she reached the end of the hall. Jean lifted her daughter's blouse to check for contusions. Below the shoulder blades she found a cross-shaped weal.

Still rancoured at the recourse to exorcism, 'Fred' took further revenge on the following Easter Sunday. Jean rose to find inverted crosses painted neatly on all her doors. The symbol was delineated in gold paint. 'Fred' had apparently used an aerosol spray taken from the garden shed. When Jean tried to replicate the painter's handiwork, she found that the glossy surface of the door made this impossible. The paint simply coalesced into globules and ran away.

'Fred' had made his presence felt a myriad times but his existence, vouched for by dozens of people who had witnessed his mysterious acts, had never been confirmed by actual sightings. Towards the end of his capricious reign, this was to change. Joe and Jean Pritchard saw him first. He introduced himself one night while they were in bed, opening their door and revealing himself as a tall, hooded figure. The next door neighbour saw him too. He was similarly described as a monk, wearing a black habit and a cowl. One night, a visitor also saw the apparition, but it was the long-suffering Diane who had the biggest fright.

One evening she was busy in the kitchen making coffee. Again, ominously, the lights went out. Diane screamed as she was grabbed from behind and dragged upstairs. Joe and Jean acted instantly and rushed into the hall. In the half light they could see Diane miming some hideous scene of assault. Pulled by a hidden power, her cardigan was held taut and unseen fingers squeezed on her windpipe. She shook her head and fought for breath, spitting and yelling. With flailing limbs her parents ended the attack and they tumbled down the stairs with Diane in their arms. Close inspection revealed red finger marks all round her neck.

The end of 'Fred' was nigh. Ironically, he was allergic to something that every schoolboy knows is highly efficacious in dealing with vampires. A lowly plant had been Dracula's undoing – and it was so with 'Fred'. One of Joe Pritchard's friends recommended that innumerable cloves of garlic be strategically placed around the house. This was done and 'Fred', as far as we know, gave up the ghost.

So who was he? There are umpteen theories, some extremely convoluted and contrived and requiring a gigantic leap in the imagination. Disturbed adolescent relationships, particularly between Phillip Pritchard and his parents, are cited as giving the entity focus, an underground stream is implicated as some sort of energising force and, without evidential provenance, one local historian affirms that 'Fred' was the ghost of a monk hanged for rape and murder on the hill that was chosen over 400 years later as the site for 30, East Drive.

Even without evidence, the theory of the Black Monk is, for me, the more compelling. Pontefract has a wealth of monastic history, much of it, I am sure, still to be discovered. The poltergeist was seen in ecclesiastical garb, he focused his unwanted attentions on a young and vulnerable girl, as he did when he executed his vile crime, and, even during his damned spiritual wanderings he demonstrated his rejection of Christ.

Remember that he caused the crucified symbol to become detached from its cross and remember that he compounded his denunciation by daubing the ultimate anti-Christ symbol – the inverted cross. Surely here we have an apostate priest?

The Black Monk has vanished, for now, but who knows what mysterious coincidences might foment his return? My advice to the good Pomfretians is to exercise care and to take out insurance against his homecoming. The premium? A clove of garlic.

9

LOST WITH ALL HANDS

The mystery of the disappearance
of the *Gaul*, 1974

Dourness is a common Yorkshire trait, the capacity of
the Tyke for enduring hardship and tragedy being
nowhere more prominent than in the fortitude and
pluck of our seamen and their kin. Statistically and in
perilous reality, fishing is the most dangerous occupation in Great Britain. Concomitant death is relatively
commonplace, mourning relatives and friends exhibiting a corresponding stoicism that brooks few public
tears. The unbearable horror of uncertainty, however, is
one facet of loss at sea that no veneer of implacability
can hide. The disappearance without trace of the entire
crew of the trawler *Gaul* in February 1974 would alone
have been a Yorkshire calamity without equal, but
couple this with allegations about clandestine surveillance operations, mysterious tales of arrest by the Soviet
Navy and the gnawing void of doubt and we have, even
for the resilient fishing community of Hull, the stuff of
nightmares.

Originally registered as the *Ranger Castor* but
subsequently renamed the *Gaul* by her second owners,
Hellyer Brothers (a British United Trawlers subsidiary),

the vessel first left her Lowestoft slipway in August 1972. A thoroughly modern, two-deck stern trawler, fitted with the latest navigational equipment, including a direction finder, a Decca navigator, a Loran navigation system, magnetic and gyro compasses, automatic steering and twin radios, she proved herself entirely seaworthy. Why then in the same Cold War period that witnessed the loss of the Gary Powers U-2 spyplane and the arrest of the prying USS *Pueblo* by the North Korean navy, had this expertly skippered and crewed trawler disappeared without trace? To many anxious shore watchers the answer was obvious.

With an all Hull complement – skipper Peter Nellist and a crew of thirty-three – the *Gaul* left the port in the early hours of 22nd January 1974. She had barely entered the shipping lanes when it was discovered that an over enthusiastic quayside farewell by a well wisher had resulted in the trawler carrying an extra man! John Heywood had not heard the calls for disembarkation, but as an experienced and conveniently unemployed fisherman he was promptly signed on as a general-purpose hand. Later that day the trawler stopped off at Bridlington and took on board a second general hand, a seaman named Tracey, bringing the final complement to thirty-six.

During the four day voyage towards the Norwegian port of Lodingen, mate George Petty was taken ill. A port doctor confirmed he was unfit to continue the voyage and he was replaced by Maurice Spurgeon, who was transferred by aircraft to rendezvous with the *Gaul* as she reached Tromso. In the almost perpetual winter night of an Arctic February, the doomed *Gaul* finally slipped her cables and headed for the fishing grounds.

From this moment on, details are sparse. For the next,

Typical February conditions on the North Bank off Norway. (Hull Docks Museum).

presumably uneventful, few days the ship went about her business, sharing the vast ocean leagues with her sister trawlers *Swanella*, *Orsino*, *Pict*, *Kelt* and 19 other craft. Religiously complying with procedures, skipper Nellist reported his position and catch details by radio at nine o'clock every morning. On the 7th February, mate Spurgeon reported an automatic steering fault, seeking advice from Hellyer Brothers' superintendent engineer. On the following day, the 8th February, the *Gaul* was spotted in rapidly deteriorating weather by William Brayshaw, the mate of the *Swanella*. After contacting the vessel by VHF radio telephone, he reported seeing her at about 10 o'clock lying beam-on to a force 10 wind. Shortly afterwards, breaching huge seas, she passed within one mile of the *Swanella* on the starboard side, heading west before the weather. Her course was plotted on the radar screen until she disappeared.

Two crew members' private telegrams, of a routine nature, to parties in Hull, were transmitted from the *Gaul* via Wick Radio between 11.06 am and 11.09 am. Then silence. Nothing was heard from the vessel on the 9th of February. The 10th dawned with still no word from the normally fastidious Nellist and, by this time, Hellyers' duty communications secretary, David Close, was becoming anxious. After trying without success to contact the *Gaul*, he raised the alarm and at 9.25 am on the 11th February, a full three days after she had last been seen, the following signal was transmitted: 'To all vessels fishing North Bank, Norway – all vessels please report any contact with *Gaul* last reported fishing North Bank. Nil reports not required.' Agonisingly, the silence continued.

Once alerted, the Bodo rescue coordination centre, south of Narvik, swung into action, organising a flotilla of ships and dozens of aircraft to begin combing a vast area of sea covering 177,000 square miles. Norwegian long-range Orion patrol aircraft and shore-based Sea King helicopters, as well as RAF Nimrods from UK bases, Norwegian coastguard cutters and several warships and part of an armada of British naval ships steaming towards the Lofoten Islands in preparation for a NATO exercise, joined the fruitless search. Despite the deployment of thousands of men equipped with the very latest sophisticated electronic, computer and radar technology, nothing was found of the ill-fated *Gaul*, and at 4 pm on the 15th February the operation was abandoned. No wreckage – not a spar, not a buckled plate, not a shard of timber – was ever found, save for a lifebuoy, eventually discovered a full three months after the assumed sinking, 18 miles off the Norwegian coast. However this was not the only mystery. There were dozens of other unanswered questions; a braying press and a justly vociferous caucus of numb relatives also demanded some answers.

Plans for a formal public inquiry were made in a climate of wild speculation and amidst repeated and vehement accusations that the *Gaul* had been engaged in intelligence gathering, the debate attracting a national audience. Some commentators even suggested that the extra hands, Heywood and Tracey, were, in reality, Royal Navy spies! The controversies rumbled on until October, when on the 17th, Mr B. Sheen QC, Wreck Commissioner, opened the inquiry in the Victoria Galleries, City Hall, Hull.

For 15 days the inquiry heard a mass of evidence, the *Gaul*'s builders, her owners, a representative of the Department of Trade, counsel for skipper Nellist and a number of the trawlermen who had been in the vicinity of the vessel shortly before her loss, all being interrogated in a determined attempt at discovering the truth. Commenting on the vexed question of spying, the advocate for the Department of Trade caused pandemonium in the court. 'This theory was based solely on hearsay but has been checked out and is incapable of substantiation. British trawlers are not used for intelligence purposes.' There was a violent response, one woman shouting, 'It was rigged for spying! You know they have it!' Some time later, a second lady fuelled the accusations, Countess Betty Von Sievert alleging that her brother, an exiled German nobleman turned *Gaul* trawlerman, had been arrested by the Russians.

Other important claims were scotched. Three women told the inquiry about a distress call they had heard whilst listening to BBC Radio Humberside on Saturday, 9th February. A music programme was suddenly interrupted, vowed Mrs Evelyn Anderson of Hull. 'A young man came on, saying "Mayday, Mayday, anybody listening, HELP", then a man was telling someone to bring a line. I could hear the sea in the background. I could feel for them. You could hear them murmuring. It sounded so real. Then the voice said: "We are lashing on the rocks. We are going over. We are going over." Then it went back to the music.' This and similar evidence from the other two women was dismissed, an explanation for the apparent distress calls coming from a radio station news editor, who suggested that the women had been confused by a highly realistic educational programme about a sinking trawler broadcast on the 7th February.

After analysing copious transcripts and affidavits, the Wreck Commissioner reached his verdict and published the inquiry findings, concluding that the *Gaul* had capsized and foundered 'due to being overwhelmed by a succession of heavy seas ... It seemed probable that the *Gaul* was lost between 11.09 am and 16.30 pm on February 8 – a period during which the weather was at its worst.' And so the official book was closed. But the controversy continued raging.

In October 1975, prompted by the continued lobbying of bereaved relatives of the trawlermen and others, Thames Television broadcast a two part investigative enquiry into the loss of the *Gaul*, paying particular attention to the recovered lifebuoy. This had been discovered by the master of a Norwegian fishing vessel and handed over to the authorities for forensic examination. Marked with the one word 'Gaul', it was positively identified by a marine painter who recognised his own lettering and traces of the previous name 'Ranger Castor' showing through underneath. The site of its recovery, far away from the presumed position of the wreckage, taking into account currents, tidal drift, wind patterns and the elapsed time, caused some puzzlement but even this, it was contended, was over-shadowed by the findings of experts at Bristol University. They announced that the lifebuoy was host to a species of microscopic plant life alien to seawater! The organisms could, the boffins insisted, only thrive in fresh water. The obvious conclusion was that the lifebuoy had been removed from the *Gaul*, perhaps by the Soviets, and later deposited in the ocean for some sinister purpose. The second television programme focused on allegations made by Stanley Kent, a retired petty officer and a former nightwatchman at St Andrew's Dock, Hull. He claimed to have seen top secret electronic eavesdropping equipment installed in two trawlers – the *Ross Illustrious* and the *Lord Nelson*. 'I took one captain a cup of tea one day and saw the equipment working,' he said. He also insisted he had evidence to suggest that a third vessel, also owned by British United Trawlers, had been similarly fitted out. Despite these sensational revelations, officialdom refused to accept any explanation for the *Gaul*'s loss, other than that propounded by the official inquiry, whose view remains unchallenged to this day.

But what was the real truth behind the mystery of the *Gaul*? Until her remains are found, and surely her skeleton will be discovered someday, albeit 600 ft down or languishing in a Murmansk scrapyard, until then all is hypothesis and conjecture. Having weighed all the hard evidence, the inquiry concluded that she had been lost to the sea. In the continuing opinion of some analysts,

A modern successor to the 'Gaul' – 'Arctic Corsair' tied up at Hull.

however, this judgement is flawed, particularly when perplexing questions remain unanswered. At the inquiry, the Department of Trade representative categorically stated that British trawlers were not engaged in spying activities and oblique reference to the absence on board the ship of naval officers, who would have operated any surveillance equipment, was contained in the inquiry findings. 'There were at that time 36 hands all told on board, all of whom were regular fishermen. There were no passengers and the Court is quite satisfied that no other personnel were aboard *Gaul* at that time.' How then did this square with the subsequent statement by William Rodgers, the Minister of State for Defence, who, although refusing to be interviewed on the television programme, admitted that RN officers had sometimes used trawlers for 'sea-going' experience. And how truthful were the findings, assessed against the illuminating disclosures in a conveniently forgotten book?

Jeremy Tunstall's acclaimed work, *The Fishermen – The sociology of an extreme occupation*, was published in 1962. A highly respected examination of the fishing industry, involving hundreds of hours of detailed interviews and painstaking research, it was esteemed by professional sociologists and was a work enthusiastically reviewed and quoted in Parliament. In one revealing paragraph the author notes, '. . . the Barents Sea area is used for training purposes by the Russian Navy – indeed British naval officers sometimes make trips on trawlers specifically to observe Russian warships at sea in this area.'

In perspective, it seems sensible to assume that the Royal Navy took an opportunistic view, installing listening devices on outwardly innocent craft operating in some of the most strategically important shipping lanes in the world. It is equally sensible to propose that the Soviet Navy itself took more than a passing interest in the ongoing NATO exercise, deploying both surface and sub-surface vessels in shadowing the carrier HMS *Hermes* and its squadron of potentially belligerent warships. Was, somehow, this mutual probing and appraisal a factor in the disappearance of the *Gaul*? I think so, although I shy away from the proposition that she was arrested and her crew incarcerated in some Russian gaol. There is not an ounce of substance to this hypothesis and it is hard to imagine an arrest followed by silence and a total absence of announcements in the propaganda war. But there is one theory, a plausible, if highly imaginative and somewhat fanciful explanation, that could hold water.

The most continually taxing conundrum in the whole tragic affair is the business of the lifebuoy and its patina of freshwater organisms and the site of its recovery, way off beam. An altogether new scenario has to be proposed to make sense of these facts.

Assume that the *Gaul* was fishing at the time of her demise. The weather during those eventful February days was bad. We know this from the reliable testimony of other crews in the vicinity of the North Cape. We also know that, despite the atrocious weather, the *Pict* had been actively fishing, because at around 3 pm on the 8th February she lost her trawl and most of her gear to a massive wave. Having been idle for some time, could not skipper Nellist also have taken a risk, taking advantage of a lull in the gale? And could not his trawl have been snagged by a Soviet submarine?

In recent years there have been several incidents involving fishing boats that were dragged under after Royal Navy boats became entangled in their nets. Could the *Gaul* have suffered a similar fate, capsizing and sinking before she had a chance to radio for help? But if this did happen, how do we explain the mystery of the lifebuoy?

Developing the theory further, imagine the 1,100 ton trawler being pulled down by the stern by a significantly bigger Y-class 9,000 ton ballistic missile vessel of the Soviet Navy. Realising that a catastrophe had occurred, the sumbarine commander would have had three priorities – to extricate his boat, to assess damage and to leave the area quickly before the arrival of NATO ships. So he surfaced, cut himself free from the sunken *Gaul*, recovered one of her lifebuoys – her maritime ID – and set course for his home base for repairs.

During the next three months the boat was under repair in a freshwater lock, a trophy, a souvenir, the lifebuoy strapped to her side. Eventually readied for sea, she was joined by her commander...but something caught his eye.

There is between seafarers a universal respect and comradeship that transcends all differences of race and creed, so might not our Russian commander have decided to honour the drowned men of the *Gaul* in one last heroic gesture? And would it be too wonderful to suppose that he returned that lifebuoy to the deep with a wreath and a prayer?

A highly imaginative proposition this may be, but in the absence of any other explanation that satisfies all outstanding questions let it suffice as a tribute to 36 brave men of the sea.

A WOMAN WHO NEVER WAS

The mystery of the skeleton
in the herbage, 1981

This is the age of certainty. Personal privacy and anonymity are no more, the all-encompassing birth to death data sciences accounting for every individual within the UK. Since the 1960s it has been virtually impossible for any citizen of this country to go unrecorded... somewhere. So what happened to the records of the lady whose mouldered remains were discovered near the top of Sutton Bank on the 28th August 1981? And why, despite the huge and co-ordinated efforts of policemen, government and local authority officials and forensic scientists does her identity remain a mystery?

The body of the unidentified woman – I shall give her the dignity of the name Laura – had lain obscured by roadside vegetation on the Scawton/Rievaulx Abbey road near its junction with the A170 Thirsk to Scarborough route. Thousands of cars must have passed the decomposing body, their occupants completely unaware that near a popular roadside picnic spot lay a corpse. The terrible secret was to be revealed at 8 am on the day before the bank holiday weekend, when the Ripon police received an enigmatic call.

A man, speaking in a cultured voice with a hint of a local accent, gave precise details of Laura's resting place near the entrance to Scawton Moor House Farm. This caller, when pressed, declined to give his name. 'I can't identify myself for reasons of national security', he said before ringing off.

Under the direction of Detective Chief Superintendent Strickland Carter of the North Yorkshire Police, the team began clearing the ground of its serried stems of rosebay willow herb to enable a detailed examination to begin. The search area was cordoned off and, with the painstaking skill of archaeologists, officers began slowly exposing the skeleton. Once fully revealed, it was left in situ for further detailed assessment and photographic recording of bone orientation by Dr Michael Green from the Department of Forensic Medicine at the University of Leeds. Other experts sifted soil samples, hoping to find clues to the cause of death and to the identity of the deceased. Preliminary on-site appraisal of the pelvic bone established that the remains were those of a female, Dr Green deducing from insect activity within the skull and surviving brain tissue, that the body had been on the ground for about two years. With due reverence, the bones were collected up and despatched to the laboratory in Leeds.

Publicity about the grisly discovery was withheld until late evening, the police calculating that a news embargo might rouse the curiosity of the anonymous telephone caller who they hoped might revisit the scene. A knot of bored detectives spent a fruitless night watching from a hideout in the woods. Some of their colleagues meanwhile had achieved more positive results.

Digging beneath the grave site, officers turned up the lid of a meat-paste jar. Close by they unearthed a single toenail. More easily retrieved, but potentially of equal significance, a discarded cardboard box full of empty wine bottles next came to light. Found on an adjacent dry-stone wall, it contained one particularly interesting bottle, its Carbonnieux label showing its former contents had been placed in it on the 3rd October 1980. Whoever had dumped the box had, conjectured the police, trodden on the grave. Had they noticed anything suspicious? An appeal for information drew a blank.

The chronology of events was further advanced by close inspection of the first find. Manufacturer's data on the jar lid showed it had been released for sale on the 6th October 1979. As it was found underneath the body, it was logical to suppose that Laura had been disposed of after this date. As for the toenail, the cosmetic company Max Factor confirmed it was varnished with a product from their 'Maxi' range. Evidential opportunities at the top of Sutton Bank were now exhausted. The task of identifying the unknown woman next fell to intensive forensic examination of what remained of her body and to dogged enquiries by the police.

Dozens of officers were assigned to the case. Early results were promising. A local stud jockey who passed Scawton Moor House Farm on daily horse-training sessions during October 1979 told police he remembered a nauseous smell wafting from the verge. He had intended to dismount to investigate but he took a tumble and was hospitalised with a broken leg. By the time he was back in the saddle the foul odours had gone. With the month of death now firmly established, investigators were able to focus in on missing persons registers and the enquiries were given a further boost by the provision of additional vital intelligence by Dr Green and other experts.

From the meagre remains, forensic science produced a remarkable description. Laura was between 38 and 40 years of age, around 5′ 2″ tall, of slim stature with dark brown hair worn short. She had dentures in her upper jaw and, judging by the discoloration and resilient coating of the teeth in her lower jaw, she had been both a smoker and a resident of an area with naturally fluoridised water. She took a size 4 in shoes, she had a spinal abnormality and she had borne children, probably two or three. Potentially, this was the most positive lead so far. Surely, nationwide publicity would elicit some response from concerned offspring?

Laura's description was circulated to other constabularies and to childrens' homes, hospitals, Salvation Army hostels, welfare organisations, institutions, clubs, and scores of workplaces across Yorkshire and Cleveland. Holidaymakers and caravanners who had used the Sutton Bank route were also contacted and door to door enquiries were made at local hotels, boarding houses, bed and breakfast establishments, campsites, shops and pubs, in the hope that one entry in a visitors' book or one vague memory of an attractive woman with size 4 sandals and painted toenails might provide the essential key to an ever-deepening puzzle.

The dental clues were pursued with obvious vigour. Intensive enquiries were concentrated in the water fluoridised Hartlepool and Grimsby areas and hundreds of dentists were sent dentication profiles and asked to check their patient records. Thousands of blank hours and hundreds of blind alleys brought only frustration, but somewhere, somehow, this woman must have left a mark. Where had she given birth? Were there any hospital or sickness records? Had she claimed child allowance? Did she have a bank account? These multiple questions led the investigators on a myriad false trails. Then one morning came a breakthrough. The new intelligence fitted the case file like a glove and the police were convinced they had a name.

During the autumn of 1979, according to Home Office records, a female inmate convicted of manslaughter had escaped without trace from the Askham Grange Open Prison near York. Her obstetric history and description – age, height, stature and hair colouring fitted the profile of the missing woman exactly. The fact that the escapee had suffered with spinal problems seemed to confirm the probabilities beyond doubt. Only one essential requirement remained. If she was still alive, she had to be found.

A prisoner on the run would be highly unlikely to volunteer any assistance to the police but in this case they had to attempt to make contact. The question was how? Most certainly, the woman enjoyed her freedom and would be alert to signs of subterfuge and entrapment. The strategists had therefore to be highly imaginative.

As she was known to be a national of Eire, it was assumed that the woman would be hiding somewhere in Ireland. Requests for her to come forward were publicised on both sides of the border in newspapers and on television and radio. The secrecy of her hideout was guaranteed by a novel arrangement. A felon knowledgeable in the routines of the charge room, she was asked to imprint her own fingerprints onto a white sheet of paper and send this undisputable evidence of her continued health to the North Yorkshire Police. They anxiously awaited the postman for several weeks and

115

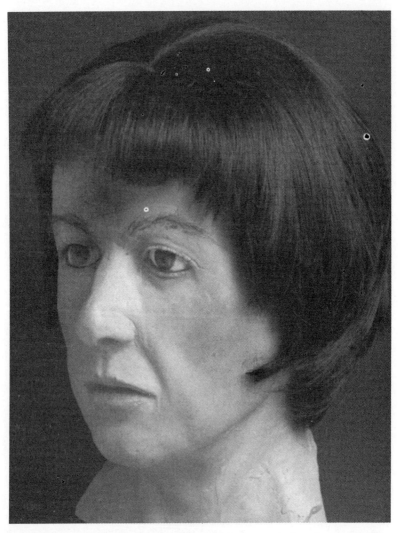

A reconstructed replica of the missing woman's head – a first in the history of crime forensics and a tribute to the Unit of Art in Medicine at the University of Manchester. (School of Biological Sciences, University of Manchester)

then, against all the odds, an envelope arrived enclosing a note and two uniquely marked pieces of paper that knocked the enquiry for six. The connection between Laura and the Irish woman had, it turned out, been purely coincidental.

Disappointed but undaunted, the task force continued its work undeflected by the lack of success and by an increasing volume of hoax telephone calls and letters. By November, all investigative avenues had proved dead ends but the ever innovative forensic scientists had one last surprise. Experts at the School of Biological Science at Manchester University had studied the fractured remains of Laura's skull and they confidently predicted that, using cranial geometry and the bone fragments as templates, they could create a lifesize and reasonably accurate replica of her head. The model was made and passed over to make-up technicians in the Granada Television Studio. They added skin tone, brown eyes and a dark brown wig and prepared the model – the first of its kind in British criminal history – for its media debut. The compelling image was widely publicised in newspapers and on television and some initially promising responses were received from the public. They were followed up, but as with all previous lines of enquiry they came to nothing.

Despite the investment of thousands of pounds and hundreds of hours of police time, the investigative process failed to produce a positive ID. The identity of the woman is not, however, the only mystery. How did she die and, more importantly, was a crime committed? Police announcements about the whole affair have been noticeably lacking in these vital details, and it must be assumed, given the incredible sophistication of modern forensic science, that this information has been determined and therefore deliberately suppressed. Why?

The police have revealed that at the time the body was disposed of it was naked – completely bereft of clothes and jewellery. This suggests that whoever was involved may have wanted to remove as many clues to identification as possible. But there is an alternative proposition. The area near to the entrance to Scawton Moor House Farm is a well-known haunt of courting couples. Laura could well have been engaged in love-making when tragedy, either accidental or deliberate, ended her life. In panic, her lover – perhaps an influential politician or a prominent businessman – might have dashed from the scene. For me, this hypothesis has more credence than that which supposes that her body was stripped elsewhere – a deliberate and premeditated act – and taken to the top of Sutton Bank for dumping. If this had been the case, the calculating mind would, in my submission, have selected a disposal site less conspicuous than a verge. Such a scenario would answer the locational riddle but what about the total failure to discover an identity? Could this be explained by suggesting that Laura was an illegal immigrant, a stateless person for whom no records exist?

In seeking answers to the numerous unanswered questions in this affair, I wrote to the North Yorkshire Police, whose case file remains open. I was particularly interested to discover the cause of Laura's death (I asked a direct question on this) and to determine if any new evidence has come to light in the intervening years. I received a most circumspect response from Detective Superintendent G.H. Chadwick. For some reason, my most burning question must remain unanswered. As for my request for examination of contemporary publicity material, the Superintendent was equally unhelpful, '...unfortunately the Press Office have weeded their press cuttings for 1981 so I am unable to assist.' Action such as this will ensure that this case will forever remain a Yorkshire mystery.

BIBLIOGRAPHY

Cassell's History of England, 1930.
Celtic and Other Stone Heads, Sidney Jackson, 1973.
The Fishermen – The Sociology of an Extreme Occupation, Jeremy Tunstall, 1962.
Green Roads in the Mid-Pennines, Arthur Raistrick, 1978.
Haunted Yorkshire, W R Mitchell, 1969.
History, Directory and Gazetteer of the County of York, Edward Baines, 1822.
The Life and Adventures of Robin Hood, John B Marsh, 1885.
Monastic Life in Medieval England, J C Dickinson, 1961.
Muker – The Story of a Yorkshire Parish, Edmund Cooper, 1948.
On the Trail of Robin Hood, Richard de Vries, 1982.
Old Yorkshire Dales, Arthur Raistrick, 1967.
Portrait of Yorkshire, Harry J Scott, 1965.
Yorkshire Oddities Incidents and Strange Events, S Baring Gould, 1874.
Yorkshire Revealed, G Douglas Bolton, 1955.
Witchcraft in Yorkshire, Patricia Crowther, 1973.

ACKNOWLEDGEMENTS

Fate inextricably links certain people to mysteries and in compiling this book I have had the privilege of using a great deal of original source material supplied by actual witnesses to these strange events. In this respect, my special thanks go to Barbara Green of the Yorkshire Robin Hood Society and to Michael Shepherd for access to his scrapbook about *A Barnsley Ballet*.

I would also like to thank the staffs of the Hull and Leeds libraries for research facilities; Ian Hartley, News Editor of the *Barnsley Chronicle* for much valuable information; the School of Biological Sciences in Manchester for use of the skull reconstruction photograph in connection with *A Woman Who Never Was* and the landlord of the Cross Keys in Old Snydale for sharing his knowledge of *The Phantom of Old Snydale*.

INDEX